LIFE CLASS

Life Class

GLYN HUGHES

Shoestring Press

Published by Shoestring Press
19 Devonshire Avenue, Beeston, Nottingham, NG9 1BS
(0115) 925 1827
www.shoestringpress.co.uk

First published 2009
© Copyright: Glyn Hughes
The moral right of the author has been asserted.
ISBN: 987 1 904886 98 3

All rights reserved. No part of this work covered by the copyright hereon may be reproduced or used in any form by any means – graphic, electronic, or mechanical, including copying, recording, taping, or information storage and retrieval systems – without written permission of the publisher.

Typeset and printed by Winstonmead Print, Loughborough, Leicestershire LE11 1LE
(01509) 213456

ACKNOWLEDGEMENTS

Extracts of *Life Class* have appeared in *The London Magazine* (February/March 2007), in *Ambit 193* (Summer 2008), and in *Tears In The Fence 47* (Winter 2007).

Two sections (with drawings) were published as *Two Marriages* by Shoestring Press, December 2007.

I must also thank those who have given me their enthusiasm and support, without which I doubt that I would have sustained the writing of this poem, and who have offered much valuable critical advice. Especially to David Pownall, Luke and Valerie Spencer, Mike Freeman, Sebastian Barker, and my scrupulous editor, John Lucas. These have diverted me away from many unprofitable bye-ways.

A special thanks must be given to Sir Ernest Hall, who has subsidised the design, production and distribution of this book.

For L., and someday for T.

CONTENTS

PART ONE
    I.   3
    II.   14
    III.   22
    IV.   32
    V.   33

PART TWO
    I.   39

PART THREE
    I.   53
    II.   56

PART FOUR
    I.   67
    II.   72

PART FIVE
    I.   79
    II.   81
    III.   83

PART SIX   Hawthorn Goddess
    I.   99
    II.   104

PART SEVEN
    I.   111
    II.   118

PART EIGHT
    I.   123
    II.   125

PART ONE

I.

1.

Caring mothers fed us bacon, eggs,
black-puddings, sausages, fried bread;
packed egg sandwiches and thermos flasks
for my friend, whom I shall call Farley, and me:
two youths who thought they had outgrown
such tenderness – of mothers also angry,
quivering without utterance
for what in 1950 they dare not say:
their fear that we were homos, poufters
in too close a friendship
for what might we get up to when
sharing a tent in the probable rain?
Throwing off our 'narrow-minded' homes
we met carrying rucksacks, tents
(ex-commando, weighed a ton)
tin cups, primus, maps, compass,
ironed pyjamas, waterproof trousers,
sketchbooks, gouache, brushes,
by the Regal Cinema –
not to join the Mods on scooters,
the Teds in what is now a coffee bar
(with *Lancashire Tripe and Cow-heels* gone).
Our eyes are filled by gaps in houses;
somewhere beyond
the city built on unfathomable fury
at any rate to us; beyond
the unforgivable, industrial detritus.
Somewhere above the crowd, to which a car
driven by the lonely or plain generous
will help us escape –
we suburban boys for the first time exploring
the elements with open, loving senses
and tutored in a scrutinising eye

by English 'nature' writers, painters:
Edward Thomas, Constable, Richard Jefferies,
Turner and D.H. Lawrence.
We know that, cold, wet, tired,
dinned with the highways' ugliness,
we'll achieve the balm of still lakes,
odours of their banks that feel the sun
and earth that feels the rain.
                                           Thumbs raised,
sometimes a van, once a Jaguar,
once crammed with sheep intended for slaughter,
once with a vicar who 'believed' in youth
especially art-students such as us
awed like him by Rembrandt and Bach,
once with a toff in an open car, (girls waved
at traffic lights along the A6),
once with a dippy old dear who invited us
up for the night (we were not taken in) –
all of them loners and talkers
but sometimes for an hour left soaking
at a roundabout was our luck of the draw
for lifts to Wales, down London way,
Cornwall, Scotland, or up The Lakes.
As on the occasion that I recall.

Wastwater was a blue and ice-eyed fiord
walled with crimson and orange bracken.
Buttermere bore a shadow sketched
as its edge cut bright water.
At dusk watched gnats sift through their dances
and from a tent door, the sun
turned leaves into seeming a bright flock of birds
nervously twitching with light.

By the time of owl-call – badger or hedgehog peeping –
I stir to flames the logs of our camp-fire
(willow spat badly, ash and beech did well)
to keep alive the smoking

embers and talk of poetry,
bombarding my friend through dusk and dark
from my battered and beloved Palgrave
(the C. Day-Lewis revision, cover soon lost).
Dead leaves now, but once a spirit guide
leading me, say, to trespass in that wood
lit by moonlight or by sparking embers
of our camp-fire spluttering in dark and rain;
or sitting out the wheel of a clear night
vertiginously peering among stars
that are peeling towards the horizon or those nets of trees.

In hazel woods at Seatoller came the rain,
its music on leaves and on taut canvas
or tearing the capes of summer leaves;
scents breathing from warmed grass
as, camping by a smoky fire
feeding it wet sticks of hazel and sycamore,
drying clothes soaked on Honister Pass
we fried bacon, black puddings, eggs,
sausages, bread, ate half-warmed beans,
half-cold porridge tainted with the smoke
that circled and smarted.
From under canvas next morning staggered sleepless
as beauty on bright wings swept by
when the mistress, or was it master-colourist
spread an explosive dawn upon the hill.
Rolling our tent up in a dewy dawn,
startled bird-chatter in the beams
of sudden light that brought
corkscrews of the rising mist.
Then wiped our billy-cans out with grass.
I hear the creak of unjointed tent-poles now,
my friend washing in the river,
me tidying up our dampened fire.

*

We, the painterly kings of feeling
caught in threads and tangles of ideals
could spend all day without speaking
not moving either, but stare
or point, we were so intimate.
Sometimes we walked the night until moonrise, moon fall.
Once came upon Dove Cottage from the Fell.
(Cold, hungry walkers, we could have been
tramps the Wordsworths remarked on more than once.)
Camped that night trespassing by the Lake.
Imagined the calm of poets' discussions,
the quiet of their reading, the quick
of their walks' alert epiphanies;
their sharing that was an awed silence
shared. And then – like ours – their garrulous
hushed indicators, *'Look! – Look there!'*
Our word for every beauty then was 'glorious!'
Glorious hills, woods fields. The word
had incantatory magic. It stiffened us with health,
resolve and vision and strength.

Sometimes, in friendship by our haven's fire
or pitching tent at the fragrant side
of a wood at dusk
we could perhaps have touched … but didn't.
Just listened. And if we spoke it was no more
than with agreeable murmurs while we heard
day birds settling, night birds coming out
among the hunting animals, we so motionless
that none took notice – not as we did of each other.

And once we met a fox. A fox arrested in the leafed light
of the forest – not exactly as if visited
by death (although a cursory glance might miss
the super-living tension of its stillness).
Then it fled, silent as a brown light.

*

Maybe it was simply boyhood
that found us strange and unexpected
paths to follow and a sense of frontier;
over the hills, a paradise
beyond our urban claustrophobia,
where instinct took us?   Instinct that found
farm-widows who brought to our tent their home-baked pies:
older women, with guile and need,
with promises and dangerous smiles
hesitating to tell their stories,
persuading us to stay – young, healthy boys –
and work (inherit?) their farms
down flower-scented lanes.
An England that Keats and Turner would recognise
where today must be
a hedgeless, tarmac-ed way
and someone defensive, private.
Places of animals and of musical birds:
time and again in Shropshire and in Wales
the eternal reliable song that did not ease
their trapped, those hinted at, adult griefs.

Or is this premature oldman-speak
in a soft shroud of sadness, but no thorns
perceived after lunch and wine?
One cat-napping with his aches to wake him,
his world reduced to the comforting moon
of a lamp on a bedside table,
waking to trace the lines of his stray thoughts?
One who – as, before dark comes,
when birds and animals peck and scratch for food –
picks his way late for spiritual sustenance
in hope that there will be built in my mind
a still pillar carved out of flux.

*

Thumbs up again down the A6
leaving blisters of fires by lakes and woods,
heat-cracked rings of stones, charred logs
(and holes in a bowling-green once
after we had pitched tent in the dark
of Borrowdale when tumbling off Scafell).
Came back with wet, wool socks,
boots holding water, stained maps,
broken thermos, unwashed pans
for mothers honoured to wash them
and parted for our different homes.

*

I've read that, to experience hell
children have had their fingers held in flame
for a second and told to imagine eternity.
Maybe everlasting joy is the same;
is love's abyss of eternal time
in moments hung on such meetings.

It would be always thus, we thought,
or, because we were so wise, would just get better
and better, until the end of time.

2.

My father, the *'Betrayer'*,
would be down town with his mistress.

A Romany and a war-time bus conductress,
her family lived in vans upon a heath
littered with scrap iron, their ponies grazing
near the bus depot where he worked.
She knew more than we ever would about camp-fires,
was so mysterious, she seemed veiled in smoke:

the essence of her dark hair,
illicit nature, or her natural pleasure.
Wild, I thought her, from the start;
not like my mother – tamed, civilised.
She was the dark-bright spirit of that watery place
we called 'The Moss'
that the canal threaded and our house looked over.
Birch trees rose there as pale lights out of pools,
pale willows bent in wands of light,
but no houses, nothing domestic
nor industrial among unstable reeds.
There heron and brown owl flew.
Carp basked and turned as if they were frying
in pans of blazingly coloured flowers.

     With swinging hips
Gertrude – *'the cheeky besom!'* – when I was eight
had cooked me ambrosial egg-and-chips
in Mam's kitchen while she was out.
My mother's apron claimed for her waist
(how lovely on Gertrude, the fall, the tie)
she desecrates Mam's new pressure-cooker
with an inch of boiling lard.
The fat is spitting, then she lays a plate
with chips and an unburned egg.
Her jaunty, *'Better than your mother's?'*
is followed by my betrayal – 'Yes!' – because it *was*.
And that was because *she'd* done it.
I've loved her in secret ever since.
'Call me Auntie Gertie', and I did.
In fact I embraced her for my anima.

At that same gas stove and that sink,
formica table, cracked linoleum floor,
her bike tucked into the almost-empty larder
to store it safe and dry,
hardboard stained for an oak-look door,
the paint grained with a metal comb –

her fortress reclaimed (this is nine years later)
disinfected with DDT
to rid it of spiders, *gypsies*, flies,
my mother (still neatly overalled from work)
in the haste of the inarticulate
(with a pause wrongly timed before the kill
thus threatening when she did not mean it –
and then her voice like the swipe of a knife –)
snapped, 'What did you two get up to –
then?'
        Unable to explain our rejoicing
I gave the worst of answers: '*Nothing much.*'

*

Both our mothers menaced their sons
through fear they would run from their destiny,
a decent job (teacher, say) that recompensed
them but had reared two rebels
escaped to their illusion of understanding
and, what we were big on then, 'enlightenment'
(the new word of our adolescence)
as if it winged out of nature or out of Bach
unaided, and only for us, from 78s
in Farley's better-class bedroom.
Cross-legged, silent, solemn as priests,
for an hour Bach's partitas and *the* Chaconne
hummed through his open window
out of his mother-polished 'radiogram'.
Or hammer blows of Beethoven and of Brahms
fragmented into 78s, the discs sliding
down as if written into the music
was that sharp *clunk* and scratching sound,
while we browsed badly-printed monographs
especially on Gauguin and Van Gogh;
those other dreamers of a Paradise.

                          'What
are they up to?'
His mother must have dreaded
to catch us *in flagrante* on the bed!
How could *she* understand the 'glory' of Bach?

So as to surprise, what she feared to surprise,
– imagining boys' white flesh against flesh
disgustingly naked – her climb was light.
She holds a tray of sweet biscuits, of frilled cups and plates
patterned with flowers like her pinny.
And – making that prettiness absurd – her frigid glare.
The last interruption we'd bare
to Gauguin and the 'glorious' Chaconne!
Then Farley slamming the door in her face.
Their mutual anger flaying like paint-stripper.

3.

While my mother is cleaning others' houses
my father is explaining why he needs love.
What could a man of his age want it for?
The wireless is tuned to the *Light Programme.*
A fire like the *Flying Scotsman's* climbs
the chimney and a fusty smell
of warmed raincoat seeps from somewhere.
Or perhaps it's the stuffing of the furniture?
Or is it the wellington boots he wears?
For him to direct buses on 'the stand'
(as they call the depot) or inspect tickets
this kindest of men is uniformed
like an SS officer or so they say
of his brushed and ironed severity
around our housing estate. Therefore the dry
pungency of overheated serge
and boots (the ones my mother polished daily).

His kindness to work-mates and his pride,
mother and I thought we could see through
for I've been taught the worst about him since
that egg-and-chips fracas at the age of eight.
Defeated or escaping, I didn't know,
but now he's hardly ever at home.
There minimal duty reigns
between my parents, spoken of as 'fate'.
('You make your bed – you lie in it.')
So to listen holds a frisson of treachery.
And he's been drinking.
'Your mother's a good woman ...' he begins,
seeming to mean the contrary.
Emotion grips him. 'If ever you should feel ...'
(Head in his hands.) 'I can't resist ...
(Head back in hands and shuddering again.)
'I 'ope you never feel such pain.
You meet someone ... and you're in *agony*.'

It was all *Brief Encounter:* the anxious rendezvous
in case they were seen or could not make it
(her husband having returned now after the War)
to *The Lancashire Tripe and Cow-heels Café* – staring
into one another's eyes,
not hearing one another's words
(well, Dad would have done the talking)
but that *'dammed blasted* music', the *Warsaw Concerto* –
then in the mind and on the wireless now –
brings those tears that my Dad's hiding.
Their lives are a picture of missed or half-missed chances,
and here is the end of things – when it isn't the end
nor even the start of the end, just the pain
of memory beginning,
intensified by the *Warsaw Concerto*.
'*I do so love you, vary, vary much,*' (Trevor Howard)
and (Celia Johnson) (posh) '*I want to die.*'

The suffering of such tendresse
is hard to take from one's father.
Yet I too have betrayed my mother
through my childish love of Gertrude.

*

Next, as always, he swoops back
to the Thirties when youths' hopes were blighted
('never to happen again')
by Unemployment, but no surrender to that!
A baker's boy, one with ideals,
he'd left stolen bread on doorsteps, gone
to Union meetings in his mother's slippers
along the Cheshire lanes he loved,
though Cheshire toffs he loathed –
by and large, he'd found, a pitiless species
known to him as teachers, vicars,
magistrates and landowners
'denying an old woman a rabbit'.
Even today he is simple enough
to ask the questions that a child might ask
and rarely get an answer to: *why,
if poverty is holy, is the Church
wealthy – the Vicar dining with the Squire?*

'We could have built a battleship,'
he said of comrades at the bus depot;
that unskilled work for outcast men
whose rusted trades would be needed again.
It's not his story, it's a generation's,
told so often that it seemed abstracted.

But not his passion for Gertrude.

Nor the story of the roses.

That's his and my mother's.

II.

1.
      It returns me to
my birth, for which they had waited twelve years
and no contraception, I'm sure of it.
But when he threatened to adopt 'a nigger',
though it's rhetoric – a socialist gesture,
'airy-fairy notions and soft talk' –
she must have thought it better to lie back
at last and 'think of England' one sunny day
on St Bee's Head in Cumberland;
under her a scent of crushed thyme;
around her, summer's essence, rasping crickets,
roaming butterflies
and the aphrodisiac stirring of the sea
evaporating its cool breath; the sound
of its erogenous rise and fall,
and birds below the screaming cliff,
gulls, auks, guillemots (she did not know what they were),
gannets, terns and skuas.
She lay until the sea
threw petals of reflected moonlight over
the shore and cliff. *Is this love?* maybe
she wondered. Or perhaps
conception had been a last attempt
to delude herself things might come right...
      ....from what?
Later, whenever I lost a girlfriend he'd insist,
'What did you do to her?'
maybe thus betraying what *he'd* done
or rather had been told he had done wrong;
some 'brutal' act (although he was not brutal)
projected on him long before.

*

My later guesswork is, she had suffered trauma
from three, or was it one, or some of three,
or did she have four
brothers? Something vile
as happened sometimes in country places;
her father with a new wife, her mother dead,
(all my grandparents dead before I knew them)
everyone blind or covering up,
yet events scattering to the winds
(Canada, Northamptonshire)
uncles I was not allowed to know,
only snaps of them, (labelled *'Sunshine Snaps'* !)
stuck with flour paste in a brown album
now turning to a dust like tobacco.

Rural poverty – for so many,
starved and crazed among plenty,
a pitiful life although a pious one –
these seem to have avoided.
Braces showing, collar-studs loose
they're dashing lads on motorbikes
ridden with fags jaunty in their mouths
as they follow 'The Cheshire Hunt'.
(Just as my young Dad enviously had).

I'm left to merely imagine so much.

*

I also see from snapshots, that had been when she changed.
Anything brightening later years,
any love she was still able to feel
survived from before whatever happened
(assuming, what seemed to have happened, had)
as if that consoled her for the barren
years by which all were dampened
after 'The Great War.'

Then she was put to live-in as a maid
for the manager of the Nestlé factory.
For mother, all is prim among the fields
of Cheshire, where cattle bruise scents out of the grass,
sorrel and mayflowers
that are processed into chocolate.
Service is delectable to her;
its rituals, then intact, stuck fast.
What was her dream? I think it was to grow old
as grandmother and great-grandmother had
in Derbyshire, in Surrey and then here;
trudging kitchens not their own,
yards, kitchen gardens not their own;
grateful for the charitable smiles,
the magisterial advice and charity wages –
the wise phrase 'cold as charity' buried
at the back of her throat
in the silence of dependence.

(Later, a snob, I would strive to belong with those
who, from Virginia Woolf to Auden,
sneered at those who made life easy for them;
and at Grammar School I learned this was a feature
of literature – Hardy, Lawrence. Even today,
Virginia Woolf's revulsion from her maids,
who made life pleasant for her, is forgiven
and not termed 'politically incorrect'.)

2.

To come back to their arrival here.
It's a council-house (called 'social housing' now)
with electric, gas, and a bath
(still an outside lavatory, though);
a nest for a denied generation
that valued new comforts and deserved them.

Though not lasting long.   When I was four
(end of a summer, I'd been playing
with Jacky Dalton, Joey Pearson, Cynthia),
glowing with the joy of sunburn
I ran at last to the shadowy indoors
where my parents sat at the wireless,
ears to webbed grill: *'War's declared.'*

What is 'War'? It was, just then,
more startling solemnity.
Margarine scraped on bread, scraped off again;
newspapers torn into squares,
threaded on string in the outside lavatory –
all this as ever, with yet more reverence.

But War improved. Excited on Dad's shoulder,
hurried out of bed to the air-raid shelter,
how comforting to look back
at the fireworks of the Blitz,
and, lit by Verey lights, a huge balloon
riding over Salford Docks!
Hitler, up there, could not reach me here!
I realise only later
how Dad, in fear, turned it into fun, and more: to beauty.

*

For my mother, here was somewhere to hang out washing
for her new baby –
in an unfortunate time for babies when breasts
and breast-feeding were unfashionable.
A child who would one day play the piano?
So she could recall how she had once done it 'at home'?
My first remembered love was to swing its candlesticks
as she banged out the *Cavaliera Rusticana*
Overture, the feeling in her head no doubt different
to what came from her gnarled, though still young, heavy hands.

Also to play at her ankles
and press the pedals of her sewing machine,
adoring its *Singer* arabesques and scrolls.
The first thing I did better than adults
was to thread her needles:
searching (to be unkind) for the eyehole of love
in her kindness that seemed without it,
enslaved to darkness that she could not express.

Though I liked to see her dance
to the wireless, but only saw it twice
(while listening to Victor Sylvester's band)
and she was not quite there
as my father, alone, pranced with exuberance
when Labour won Election
after The War – its damage
seeming buried in the rubble of sixty million lives.

3.

There was a long garden. Its manure
was horse-droppings scraped from the canal towpath,
or barrowed from the farms.
I recall being wheeled on top of it, over the bridge
where the doomed soldiers sang at night
after they had been thrown out of the pub;
and charioteered past thistles on the 'Croft'.
Rows of spuds, beans, cabbages.
Rhubarb forced under buckets where I peeped
to see the shoots, as pale as nestlings
in their darkness, and as vulnerable.
Currants ... a daisied lawn ...
 ... lilacs at the side. Large irises –
cups in which bees and black-flies climbed,
endlessly climbed and fell – in a long bed.
(Dad, in my mind, still lifts spuds with his fork:
caught in the aspic of memory. That tang also,

though whether of soil or naked
potatoes revealed, I did not know.)
                    Also, his pride of roses –
emblem of what he'd felt, and fingered perhaps –
I doubt if he ever saw it – at St Bees –
flowering thick and reaching to the roof;
the street's pride as well, a world of pink
petticoats this child could stare through to the sky.
Petals that Cynthia next-door boiled for 'scent'
in her kitchen, or ours; both anyway tanged with *absence*
like all other houses during or after the War.

*

For Mam's new start, her baby filled the void
of a dream sown by the cinema,
and by *her* rose at St Bees. A child
with a head of fair curls!
A child – I think she hoped – less a boy, more of a girl.

So perhaps he knew something that I didn't
(making him sometimes throw me challenges,
roughly tousling my fair, mannered curls)
of what she wanted and it frightened him?
Perhaps that was what they had first quarrelled over?
Maybe it was her desire to emasculate
and claim, appalled and shocked him?

Her nightmare of the male came out one day
when, wheeling her bicycle through the gate
between irises and lilac, (the sun upon
privet, sweet-williams, lavender and rose)
she found me shorn; returned to a brutal male.
Is it too strong to call this 'another rape'?
What matters is how she felt.
I recall her silence, wanting those curls back,
and her tight mouth as she gets brush and pan

for the blond floss which mostly blew away
and that made more irritating his excuses
for her lost child that she does not answer;
his bluster – his, 'damn-fool cissy!'

Five more years of simmering hate
at last erupted.
A day came when she had nothing to do,
it seemed. (Unusual for her).
Weekend – Dad at work – she sat and mooned
and for an hour pulled at her finger-ends.
(A habit, as if to snap her pain from them;
one she pursued, it seemed to me, for hours.
I'd go to bed at night and she'd be doing it;
I'd wake, she'd put my cereal out, still doing it.)
Next, kneeling thoughtfully at the back-door step, she sharpened
her carving-knife for next day's Sunday roast
with – once more – that startling viciousness
and savage motion as for her finger-ends.

Now she's decided. With few words
she took me out to fell *his* roses.
A day was soaked with broken flowers
and whipped-down, dangerous tentacles,
snaked, tangled, on the lawn;
with stubborn anger … then the burned briars;
blue smoke curling round the house. No more
a tunnel of roses gone wild at our door!

To revenge her angel-child, she took his rose.

He came home to the scorched earth of the lawn
and I to the end of my childhood.

4.

Afterwards the, first neglected, next ignored,
overgrown garden became *my* world,
an escape from the damnation of that bitter house.
Remote as Africa, strangely creatured
and much stared at,
its stormed and broken plants were a sea surrounding me.
On summer nights were hundreds of moths
(how to trap them in a jar with honey
I read in *The Childrens Encyclopaedia*)
that swirled out of weeds to the lights of windows
and by morning had turned to brown dust
over their rainbowed, inner wings.

And earwigs. (Jacky Dalton said
that those demonic insects with their horns,
if you were unwatchful lying in the grass,
crawled into your ear and next your brain
to drive you insane.)
Bats … (where did they come from? Where did they hang all day?)
… black bits of burned paper that skipped in the dusk.

Barn owls that glided out of my school.
Animals mazed the garden with their paths –
voles – and a hare once – as secretive
as I who laired in its air-glazed shadows.

*

I remember how I listened to a thrush
and scrutinised, through stalks and grass
taller than me, a light
of sunset over canal and Moss
where Gertrude was banished.

Confusion of woman with 'Nature'!
What is divine for a growing boy

is the feminine, that cooks its tea,
ties its shoelaces, butters its bread,
or sprays the kitchen with DDT
in a furious cycle of cleansing.
A spirit magical, numinous, served and worshipped
but ultimately not reached.
A woman presence missed (what woman was it?)
in houses absent of women during the War;
and even through my cycle rides and walks.

III.

1.

In teenage years when my inner love is forming,
terrifying, lovely, seeming behind a screen
of cobweb or of silk, translucent, floating,
only visible when stirred in a draught –
when it is shaping the image I saw at times
in girls and called it 'love'
(or wished it was) – I catch
 my father slipping out of the door
of a chemist's that has a 'Durex' sign
then into *'Lancashire Tripe and Cow-heels'*
where he meets *my* love – Gertrude.

He treats her to tripe and chips
while I (my *Palgrave* as usual in my pocket)
watch through the window
of the snack-bar opposite. I'm unseen as God –
they are so absorbed in one another. He
is in a suit that I know smells of camphor. She,
no longer an 'Esmerelda', is on the town
and wears a pink, transparent raincoat
(as if she isn't rose-tinted enough)
the liquid glide of that Fifties' new stuff, plastic,
strange-lovely – as had been her fall of apron once –

and scattered with rain-pearls. Real nylons now
(not wartime painted-on) and black court-shoes;
while under the baleful, blue and white cow
painted on the *Tripe & Cowheels* window, I can glimpse
her stocking-tops that I'd die for;
die (as I thought then) none other would.
And, though I can't pick up her scent from here,
I think I can, imagining it clearly,
as through my virginal palpitations,
wonder and envy, I see them *laughing*
and guess how he feels
with 'something-for-the-weekend' before they sneak
next door to the Regal Cinema.

*

So this was why – years earlier – kneeling at the spot
chosen for my forced pissing and praying
beside the chamber-pot
(face level with the white, white coverlet;
sharp scent of starch in nostrils; owls or cats
screeching outside, and moths drawn in
to flicker like my own dark demons) – mother
had demanded I forget Dad in my prayers.

2.

Another memory – oh I would rather not! –
is of the prison of the desperate bed
I shared at puberty with my father.

As un-divine as anything could be
was my parents' bed moved to my room,
my single one shifted to hers;
Dad sullenly bolting them, she stiff and stern
with victory. (No money in them days –
where did his go to? – for new beds.)

This was the condition under which she'd stay
and not go back to live-in 'maiding';
possibilities she'd explored, offering
life in this house, next in that one
(no frost of bitterness there to blight
shoots when they begin to grow)
but not stayed long before she was dissuaded.

Queening it in her distempered room
(one year switched from pink to a sad blue,
next year back to pink again)
and still pursuing her duty,
'tea' on the table according to his shifts,
his wellingtons polished, uniform pressed,
his shoulders brushed before he went out,
(dandruff and hair picked carefully off)
my mother's revenge was to put him there,
in what was 'our', not my room, now.

Her life was less a life than a wreck
of bits that had survived the storm
of her conquered, then abandoned, marriage.

One exchanged for her other call,
the one she loved, in which she moved
through rooms as a daily maid;
awed, yet seeming to screen
happy self-knowledge behind a smile.
    It was as if there shone
a light within her and I saw
not direct light of love then but its parchment shade.

*

One summer's dawn – it is four a.m. –
woken by the songs of birds,
I catch my mother at the door downstairs.
Even at that hour she is dressed for work;

dreamy and heart-aching
for the beauty of morning, her mind reaching
over the awakened horizon
(sheds, gardens, and a swathe of fields)
to where bird-song was wrung
from willows by the broken-banked canal
and exploding out of dense trees in the Park.
'Listen to the Dawn Chorus!'
she whispers – so much quieter than the birds
and posh, like on the wireless;
in love with it, her face all smiles;
in awe at that great orchestra.
Until in a dribble of song it stopped.
And it was truly weird, the way it stopped.

3.

For one last night (I didn't know that, of course)
before sleep I heard Dad go
to my mother's room. His begging. Then her iron
refusal. Though it was soft as a dove's,
repeated and repeated, I was frightened,
yet crept to the bathroom to hear more clearly.

The weight of his progress back to our room.
His small change poured onto that scratched dresser
abandoned to us, and then the shuffle
of heavier metal – his depot keys,
as usual, though now seeming heavier.
Conflicts of hate and love taint the air!
Squinting, I glimpse the shining bakelite
of his black *Inspector* cap and its gold letters,
always seen, on his head, or in the 'hall'.
(Even sometimes when he's been to my mother's room –
if he called when unable to wait after work.)

I hear the sigh on his nicotined breath.
Then I sense *failure* oozing from his pores,
in the sweat of a father who was too close to me
especially in our common love –
the rivalry for which I hated him:
love for the worshipped Gertrude.
I wished I was somewhere else and someone else.
In guilty fantasies of pain and punishment,
I wished that Mam and I had left.
Had left for *anything – anywhere.*
This would last until I ran away –
at eighteen years of age?   At twenty one?

By morning all between them's changed, I saw.

4.

It was one of those summers throughout which it rained.
Rain hung rather than fell, was green or grey,
depending where, and no such thing
as a dry lawn or an un-puddled road.
The laden trees were vast as Victorian ladies
sagged and heavily gowned in the parks.

We came to that house – I doubt I'd find it now –
tall, Edwardian, with at its top
the nest of an attic 'flat'. And a tower.
Could I see myself there, in quiet but for rain,
bird flight and song, (that wasn't as today,
but was loud as a Romantic orchestra)?
Such an aloof semi-secret appealed – a place to hide guilt
when escaping my father who didn't yet know
the devastation that my Mam and me had planned.

Went home. There for slow hour after hour
Dad reaches for cigarettes. Gertrude's name
comes up again, again. I narrowed my eyes.
Even today I can feel the creases

of hate at the corners of my eyes;
not having done this before, (seen it on film)
yet needing so much to hate
(that I did not feel), to take one side
(my mother's, and that's decided)
and to do so, thinking mostly of that tower.

We left. For days I floated loose
in the aura of a mother's magic to summon
what she desired; to summon up this place
where she could be affectionate,
tenderly caring for what was not her own;
a mother, now. As I dithered in her spell,
Dad visited twice – contemptuous, nervous; an S.S. call
in the kitchen that seemed as big as a church
(it had eau-de-nil walls and dark green cupboards)
that made him in his un-brushed uniform seem small.

He tried to refuse to talk while I was there.
The second time, he failed.
He spoke of life, of love, of new leaves, of resolve.

Mother ran down her routine of sweet tasks.
(She's tough.) I climbed my tower briefly,
my soul in fragments – some left on that floor –
then we went back home.

5.

Most nights I calculated so as to be
in peace before his unhappy body loomed
and we lay back to back; two shades of the undead,
father and son in separate dreams.
(We might have been in the same dream, too.)
My secret acts, or what I thought of as,
caused small vibrations in the bed.
He would roll and snort like a stranded seal.
What is he doing ... is he doing <u>that</u>?

Silence and stillness drop like a steel door.
He smokes a *Capstan* fag, 'Full Strength'.
(He said all other cigarettes were tasteless.)
Coughing, panting. The red tip glows.
And that other scent – *is it from Gertrude?*
I *bet* we are both thinking of Gertrude,
tits thrusting in her mac; her egg and chips.
'Son …' he begins, then stops and coughs.

*

His shifts are 'six till two' and 'two till ten'
alternate weeks. His early start
is best for me, when he rises at five
and walks to unlock the office and the garage
of The North West Road Car Company.
Three hours to watch and listen to the dawn!
Sheets and pyjamas stained,
fantasies whirl my brain;
lapses into beauty and then pain
that render me stirred, then tired.

My mother before her work
comes in with cereal, tea.
(Walls pale blue this year reflect cold light
on the drabness of nothing renewed
where there is no love.)
She feels she must do this – somewhat impatiently,
and who can blame her?
But what I thought of her and she of me –
especially whether this was love or duty –
are thoughts unspoken.

While Dad and I would hardly speak for weeks –
now that there was so very much to say.

6.

My other secrets, or so I thought –
my diary, and my Keatsian poems
(or was it more from Richard Jefferies?):
*'Migrants are flying high, they pass
unseen and noisily through the night'*
and my confessions – of the less embarrassing sort –
'What would I do without you, Diary!...'
*'...Alma is altogether too good.
When I move my hand towards her breast
she stops me...'* and, *'None
understands why I'm unhappy'*
instead of hiding them in a biscuit tin
rusting among the garden weeds
I should have told them, been a Blakean
angel-youth uttering truth.
Shocking it would be but next delivering
them into innocent light.
'We have to do something ...'

They might then have observed how often
and worryingly their only child escaped
alone on rambles and on cycle-rides.
So as not to be in, I was out.
(And I've never lost that habit.)
How I fretted for the sunlight
or wild weather when I was indoors!
Then in one blind –
-ing moment I realised I *wasn't* confined!
Could walk out and what was to stop me?
Merely to step onto a bare field ...
that liberation of space was enough.
(But it would not be bare, for there'd be flowers;
in winter there'd be scattered straws, gold;
in the dark, beetles, stars, and moths;
the beetles like metal, the moths like ghosts).

The prosperous, fertile, loving countryside
was a sensual mother, I believed unlike my own.
To be in that embrace was all that mattered.
There'd be a price,
but later. I was free at least for a day,
and every gull that was blown inland
and cried of its distant sea
dragging the ocean in its call,
and every sparrow even
(there were many sparrows then)
and of course the larks
were metaphors all, you will say. And yet
I'd not learned that from literature
for they were archetypes of nature rising
in me from that well I did not yet know was there.

*

I followed the towpath where the barges
drifted to Runcorn;
leaning on their tillers, large, peaceful women
(I never saw a skinny one), the horses led
by men with kerchiefs on their heads,
and children playing on the loads of coal.

Their stealthy float across the countryside
echoed my trespass through the fields,
secretive for fear of 'Grassy';
a mythic guardian, leaping out of hedges,
that all the kids described
(hissing the sibilant danger of his name;
the *hiss* of his very shadow, so it seemed)
as thin as a snake, and green, and fast, and wild.

*

Along lanes that penetrated the womb-depths
of Cheshire, maybe a farm-labourer
with time to take an interest
showed me wild birds' nests.

Once, a German prisoner
loosed at the War's end to work on farms
took me delightfully to spy
by private hedgerows on wild creatures.

And my poems grew out of this:
a skill to creep unwitnessed into barns,
and on the unsuspecting deer at dawn;
a secret act of secret ways.
Though lines came from an inner need, it seemed
I found them in the hedgerows and the copses
in silent, timeless, entranced pauses.

I also learned (and learned again from books)
how pitilessly wet this England can be.
That's what the land-labourer knows,
and the outcast sliding (like me) by the hedgerow
seeking birds' eggs or herbs to stew.
The poacher netting pheasants from a tree
knows it; and the desperate ones, failed by stars to light them
passed man-traps and gamekeepers –
not safe from the savagery of Old England.
Ancestors all, that I feel in my blood.

Light-hearted and light-headed with joy,
I had not yet absorbed the lesson
that love of nature may render one dysfunctional.
One perhaps ends up in a battered van
or a listing narrow-boat splattered with graffiti:
'Stop the war' (with this?) and 'save the planet'.

Or one ends with too many kids in a yert,
divorced maybe several times over
with unresolved legal papers,
shifting addresses, then no address,
dangling a crystal to divine one's fate.

IV.

1.

After one night in a straw-littered field
near Worcester (even the field was glittering with stars:
they were cattle-stirred straws, and moonlit wings of flies)
found dumped near the Long Barrow
on Cleeve Hill, *a Romany's vardo*!
The caravan's wheels and the bogeys
fine, bits of crimson and gold
still on them, fiery;
one shaft split, its tarred-canvas top
cracked, snagged on thorns –
thorns creamed with flowers, do I remember,
or was that in the Spring after?

When I returned with my five pounds
saved by weeding rockeries –
eyes level that winter with frosted plants,
or, soon, with centipedes and grasshoppers
(yes, there were grasshoppers in those times),
rooting out dandelions and couch-grass,
face inches away, worshipping the glow
of small flowers, of saxifrage suns
(work for the doctor's wife who had given me Palgrave) –
                    nails broken, hands
gladly humbled by the earth I loved
to gain a longed-for heaven.

Cycled back to Cleeve one hundred miles
taking what I'd bought with gardening money:
secondhand poetry and some tools.
Dreamed of one day bedding my first woman,
my own Gertrude in that caravan there.
Dreamed of a hedgeside life, that dwells in grass, that touches air.

Found charred wood and blackened bolts
in a grass circle grown again long and fresh –
from the centre of which a hare leapt up.
For a startled second it stretched upright, then fled,
kicking its heels, and paused to look
back from the dead centre of its field.

Was it the spirit of those hedge-side dwellers
I'd dreamed of joining
and whose souls I could not restore –
but it could?
Where do Romanies go when they die?
Not into church grounds – I've never seen that.
Why not into the souls of hares?

Its ears were pricked questioning again from the edge of the wood.

V.

1.

Though sex was undiscovered in those days.
No-one knew it, only courtship,
say a breast cupped when leaning by a wall,
or a back seat at the cinema.
It was a sigh in the long grass
quiet as air hissing from a tyre
and pressure below of an organ unfolding,
then Margaret's or Alma's wondering stare
at the 'accidental' fire, most terrible for girls.
It was meetings at a station or from a bus
with hope of love on bright days, fading
as the feet of rainbows fragment –
spoilt by the dire knowledge that, apart
from throwing their virginity away
the main thing girls would not do
was come with us.

But, before puberty, a power
discovered not only in girls but in women
long passed virginal and not
beautiful perhaps, but sexual,
a neanderthal sex mixed with fear,
was maybe my displaced, Oedipal
'dream of fair (or more truly, powerful) women'.
The causes must be many.
Awe at mystery, for one. Awe
at the power my mother had to rule
my guilt-whipped father with denial.

2.

To start with: my alcoholic piano-teacher –
a gorged python with shrill temper
who takes my mother's hard-earned half-crown.
Necklaces gleam like raindrops on her breasts
as she crashes among her crates of gin and wine,
weeps in the dark glades of her furniture
and staggers in the hall where hubby brings the coals
to her bottle-littered alcove
by the fireside in her stinking room
hung with engravings: 'Captive Andromache'
and 'Come Into The Garden, Maud'.
Tenth client of the day (so she informs me –
teeth clenched, and her lips
foaming with anger, or maybe it's only froth)
I'm not her favourite, I cannot be,
and she must need a double gin
to face my unpractised 'Farmyard Sketches'
that reduce her to screams and tears.

Did she sometimes cuddle or only scream
at hubby too? I don't doubt that 'Miss' Walker
had a feeling heart.
Perhaps she was Dvorjak's *Rusalka*:

the secret nymph who wished she was
a normal woman to be loved;
gentle, believed in; most of all, loved.
Perhaps she sometimes sat in that garden
(where I'd parted with anticipatory fear
the dusty ivy and her vicious roses)
with husband and a glass of gin?
(There was a bench, some grass.)
Why did he marry her, why stay?
They said it was for her money
but I wonder.

*

The ladies at those houses where Mam served.
We had Odyssey'd two miles, by broken fences,
gapped privet-hedge and other shabbiness
of social housing (other women too, on foot, on bikes;
and a long walk for me, aged seven or eight;
yet one that torched me with its magic)
to reach where there were overarching trees
and this sedate mystery of the shrouded houses.

A soft twilight on mossy lawns and tracks
for ladies of an old Empire – a different species,
perfumed differently, moving (well, gliding) differently,
accepting with grace what service there still was;
matrician and remote, as in a Roman province
when life had changed – and they had not realised –
for them and for houses turning into flats.

Mrs Behrens (most days and some evenings)
who'd returned from Africa with her 'native'
carvings displayed – the 'clean' ones – in glass cases.
The doctor's wife on Fridays, Saturdays.
We entered their homes (as for music lessons) by back doors
where only these were at home
among their Fabergé frou-frou and their artifacts

unlocked for my mother to dust.
Dressed in Norman Hartnell and, soon, Janet Reger
(as I knew because my mother ironed it)
they were sensual as my mother wasn't
(and encouraged my poems later, as Grammar School didn't).
Absorbed by washing pots here, Mam hummed quietly
but enjoyed more changing water for the flowers
that a gardener brought in daily,
or straightening curtains with more love
and care than she showed at home.
Here was the chasm where her tenderness vanished.

Also, when I followed to the twin bedrooms,
she with a sexual smile that this child recognised
(unique as it was – and how I wanted
her to let hair loose, be flirtatious
like Gertrude, wear black stockings and be outrageous!)
hinted at why there was a door between.
I'd no idea what it was she meant
but grasped the portent, therefore the content.
'Money doesn't make you happy,'
we often said. Maybe not but certainly it made 'you',
in a life clearly charmed,
healthy, elegant, and competent.

*

Yet soon to be sociable meant
denial, and puberty's grubby thoughts.
Meant shame at our council-house estate,
and at my mother's hands
wrinkled in sacrifice to soap, to scrubbed floors,
and to hours at the sink for others' sakes –
my shame, that shames *me,* today.

Though I had to get her off my chest,
as she had to get me off hers.
      Even until I'm seventy there's that missed breast.

PART TWO

1.

Prompted to advancement by my mother –
proud of him for once – when I was ten
Dad had been promoted to inspector:
'Inspector Ewes' – in that smart uniform,
black, Nazi; with a hinged clipboard
and bands to hold his papers.
Not wage-paid anymore, but salaried.
He accepted though it enticed him from
the Transport and General Workers' Union
that he'd given his passion to and had led
with Bert Southern through a Thirties' strike,
they both being 'dangerously' articulate.
But the Union was limited to wage-earners.
(How often was that story enacted?
'They take you over,' he said later
about OBEs, and Hugh Scanlon's –
president of his Union's – knighthood.)
He did it for my mother,
though one day he grew wiser.

Thirty or forty cheerful men
who had their reasons to miss the War
(their age – like my father – mostly)
one or two who came back after
and a few women like Gertrude – the captive-wild,
as women among men were in those days,
wearing trousers too and smoking;
plus three who were only spoken of as 'Inspector' –
Roberts, Ewes, and Southern
(yes, he too had been bought over)
ran the L-shaped 'stand' – the depot –
around two sides of the cycle shop,
'Wheelers', by the Railway Clock.

2.

Dad's office where he took me as a child.
He holds my hand with love and pride.
One high, steep desk to lean on in a shed.
The tickets with which it is lined
are pink, yellow, off-white, curling in racks
that are sprung tight as the mouse-traps that he tried
and baited for the last job of his shift
before he took the keys and walked back home
(or visited Gertrude?)
A telephone. The handle, he impressively
spun to generate electricity
for his first task after emptying the traps.
(Mice swinging like lead weights by their tails.)
The dirt and smell of money
gathered in small change, in filthy bags.
Hands print-grubby too from tabloid papers.

They loved my Dad.
(That was a surprise. In fact, a shock!)
They'd made him Chairman of the Social Club
to compensate him for his loss of Union.
Like many a working-man with no *realpolitik*
he was trapped in that mistake:
faith in kindness that made him vulnerable.
(Stalin and Hitler did not reach Altrincham!)
He pretended to be untroubled
at the bar and at the snooker table –
though still short of happiness and of cash.
(And Gertrude described him, after he died –
years later when I met her – as 'a man apart.')

When mother finds the Durex in his pocket
has that to do with both
the unhappiness and no money? There's a row.
Next, he steals that five pounds from her purse,
which hurt her for ever, and which he denies.

A stranger calls – a shaming money-lender
to assess our home – and Dad tells yet more lies.
A trap of the meanest sort has sprung.
It has *him* by the tail now.

3.

In loneliness he repeats his stories.
Inspector Southern,
a tall, quiet intellectual, I remember,
(what vocation had he been thrown out from?
I didn't think to ask that, then)
who lectured on Darwin and on Marx
to church groups and to Women's Institutes,
was crushed between two reversing buses.
Taffy – a driver – pretending to be blind
and Billy – his conductor – pretending to be deaf,
('comedians', both) shouting to Taffy
on Cheshire lanes, 'Turn left,' and 'Mind that bike,'
engendered a passenger riot and were sacked.

My father in a staff-car was once whisked
to Eisenhower's H.Q. – so he said,
to 'organise transport in the event …'
Was it true? Near Knutsford I could show
the house, its paddocks, trees and shrubs,
gravel drive and the stream curling by
willow trees and meadow-sweet,
but it was Patton's H.Q. and not Ike's.
However, I loved the fabulous tales
and Gertrude (in love) believed him I am sure.

Though she lost her job at the end of The War
and, when her husband returned,
surrendered her serge trousers and her badge
(partially her lover too) – as it happened,
at the time the North West Road Car Company

was, in a fashion, nationalised.
('In a fashion' is Labour history!)
'You'll notice once again this bus is late.
That's because we've been swallowed by the Metro
who don't give a bugger!' another 'comedian'
shouts to his passengers and is sacked.

4.

After thirty years my Dad retires
to puzzle even more about a world
'beyond any power to understand'.

They're bickering, but often loving now
in quiet ways. Is that enough?
(Where's Gertrude gone?
One day I'd find out – but I did not know.)

All, that came to nothing's, done.
All's said that made no difference.
A decade younger than me now,
they're watching tele while they wait to die.
Violent action and a lot of tits
on the room's altar are tutted over
in place of toffs and capitalists.
Mother in front of tele sees
the array of napkins, cutlery and plates,
in *Dickens* from Pinewood or Jane Austen later
and *who does all the washing-up?* she'd say.

Dad walks most days to the Social Club.
That's as far as he goes now.
(Does he meet Gertrude there?)
There's no more rambles for Dad and me
when along the car-less, Cheshire lanes
among flowers and butterflies he talks sincerely

to a mere boy about the pains of love
and of his dreams (for my mother to reverse).
In those earlier days we'd call
at 'Aunty Hilda's', 'Auntie Sue's',
a harem of 'aunties' where the crews
along the bus routes used to pause
at Rhostherne and at Leigh
(lonely war-widows – not tarts –
why would he take a child unless they knew?)
to sit politely as they made
tea that I enjoyed less than I would lemonade
and – so used to gossip – disappointed
that nothing to prick my ears about is said.
Perhaps silence measured that they understood
him in ways they could not talk about to me?
Other women (and men too)
in those days would come to gates.
Out of gardens, orchards,
they'd bring 'a bit of something' – cakes;
parkin; cheese and pickled onion;
the passengers content it seemed to wait.
In that old-fashioned, country way –
where everyone seemed glad of strangers coming –
on seeing something that he liked,
flourishing lupins – *roses* – beans,
Dad would pass a compliment,
trouble to toss it over a hedge
perhaps aware this person could be dead
without having heard such kindnesses.

In the end Dad ceased to expect
fruits from his articulated emotion –
as happened in novels he read through the night
by H.G.Wells and Henry Williamson.
So I remember silences:
infinite and more articulate
shadows behind home's arguments
that were brief, yet sharp as broken glass;

brilliant shards until they were sullied, lost –
pieces of discontent, at peace at last.

Silence and sin seemed interchangeable.
'You don't know what he was like ...'

My mother pulling her hands again as if to draw
pain out of her fingernails once more,
still angered by the sin
of his lifelong loving out of wedlock:
especially a *gypo* from The Moss.

5.

We never had that final conversation:
*Dad, you've been as good a one
as you've had <u>chance</u> to be.
No need to fear you'll be alone.*
I waited too long – thinking only now
of his fear of breaking down in pain
with no recovery, only a descent
to that much written-of door
that in truth is maybe blocked?

Collapsing after posting me a letter:
*'Thank you for Christmas. See you soon, I trust.
All our love, Mum, Pop, and Nigger'*
(that being their black cat)
received the day after he died
(he'd felt poorly, went in the bathroom –
the last Mam saw of him – and died).
She never told me how she'd felt.
Just hand-snatching grief for *her* own life.

Though others were different.
A crematorium on the Moss
(the only building on his love-haunted waste)

had its long path lined
by three bus-loads of his comrades.
Ninety men, silent when Mam and I walked by.
(Guiltily: I thought because we'd not been kind.)
Some old, many too young to have known him –
a legend from the kinder wing of The Left --
they'd come here straight from duties,
and uniformed. (I never learned how to that date a Union
retained such power to commandeer its buses!)

But Gertrude – where was she?

6.

Van Gogh compassionately drew hands
worked to tough threads yet knuckles swelled.
Rembrandt too, and I could understand,
for they'd portrayed my widowed mother's hands
that I stare at through my visits.
Mothers are our light while they wear pretty dresses
(though mine rarely did, but she sometimes tried)
then they become
old rags afraid of death, of everything,
nodding to sleep by gas fires,
our most egoistic selves reflected in
our graduation photos on their dressers.

Often I sat in educated, refined
distaste for the composite, factory stuff,
plastic, hardboard and later, mdf
for which they (well, it was she)
had cast out tables, sideboard, even the piano
that wasn't played by anyone now,
not even by visitors from Church;
while she, I believed, would never understand
why (fooled by the Romantics, she'd have thought,
had she been educated) I was fond

of the rural life that she'd escaped;
loved soil-sift through my hands,
smell of sawdust, grain in wood
(say) cast up salt-bleached on a beach,
or a marigolds' gold next to the blue of cornflowers
that I must go back and forth to for hours.

Sensuous joys that now I know, of course,
she had felt (and *perhaps* she had forgotten?)
but I didn't see it then
despite Mam's tales of sitting by that river
having her father to herself (for once).
                              Despite that flicker
of girlhood brightening sometimes as it creases
the edges of her grey eyes. Despite St Bees.

She – as thin as her wedding ring is, from scrubbing
(the two ground down together by her skivvying)
as usual tidies, irons, and cuts thin bread;
adds *Spam*. (For egg-and-chips 'Is what they call,
'*day classay*'.') Or dusts the Queen Mum on the wall.
I think the Queen Mum's there to annoy my Dad,
even now he's 'gone'. How similar
Queen Mum and my mum are! The wave, the smile,

as she will smile the last time that I see her –
when she does something strange.
Watching me go (and even that's strange for her),
from my taxi to the airport I see her
pull aside the nylon curtain
(too white, and with the slithery feel – I know –
of frog or jellyfish) – enigmatic.
Thinking it is too late to say what she
had always in any case been unable to say?
Her pride in witholding – was it all she had?
Her image then is imprinted on my brain –
her whole life of love unexpressed, or rather, denied, in it.

(Had I been more awake, I might have seen
a life of love pained into silence there.)

'I'll see you soon,' I'd lied.
We knew that Greece would claim me for a year.
Both knew by instinct that I would stay.
She, life-tutored in betrayals and lies,
sealed me in mine with her tiny smile
that I'd seen often, especially of late.
Ghostly, you might say, not in the present;
her pristine, unsullied awareness again intact;
as maybe she'd looked at me when I was a baby.

7.

Two years to the day after Dad she collapsed,
in that same room. While I was in Salonika
a neighbour had knocked because she wasn't in Church.
Called the police. They and a health inspector
dealt with what one reads of sometimes in the paper:
a woman three days dead and no-one saw,
her fluids leaked on chair and floor.

Four days later when I arrive
the ironing completed before she died
hangs starched upon a rack.
Officials cleaned up, but there's the stained carpet,
and furniture the house-clearance company
will only take away because
they 'didn't want to waste the journey'.
Clothes, hers and also Dad's
'Sunday best' (though he loathed the Church)
(that camphored suit she'd kept) I send to Oxfam.
(I've kept my graduation photo from her dresser.)

I witnessed a gypsy's funeral once, the caravan
and contents going up in flames;

children and women gathered round
the men who stirred the fire upon The Moss
with spars of wood or iron.
No laments, just fire-lit faces
and shawls clutched against the dark behind.
But nothing sanctimonious.
I thought: one could do worse.

8.

Such as go to that Crematorium on The Moss;
the very place her gypsy-rival haunted.
So I took her ashes to the bluebell wood
by the Lake she'd shown to me,
with its sacred privacy of far-water
owned by a Lord away shooting in Africa,
on cycle rides separately from Dad
and I planted one hundred snowdrops there
in her strangely-warm still, fine and light grey ash;
the heat of which I feel on my hand right now,
and is as close as I can get to love.

Others' mothers died so I know how they felt
and I confess to feeling none of that.
I could not love her – or could not find my love –
the greatest sin; a pit, I did not know then
I'd all my life not fill – turning to 'nature' for it –

 having to pay with guilt, and with the thought:
does primal abuse unfold through generations?

*

I've blamed her often for her non-love
of Dad and me. Now I'm sure I'm wrong.
Anyway, what are flaws
other than gifts we cannot deal with;
gifts driven underground and lost, therefore?

And I am close enough to my own death
not only to wonder who will feel it, but how,
and want to live to save you, Liz and others
(something else that's quite ridiculous)
from that oneiric ache
that seems – that does in fact – go on for ever.

The sense of waste: a dreamlike underpinning
pushing back my familiar, yet no longer familiar
land on the way to the Crematorium.
That sense of wasted time enwrapping them
that makes grieving people awesome.

PART THREE

I.

1.

Heaven. Miss Bennion had described how it came after
the grave, its 'empyrean' (she called it) blue
as my mother's room's distemper,
(changing it each year from pink to blue
as if unsure which mood is true.)
There we'd sit around the feet of Jesus
in His sandals that looked bought from Marks and Spencer's
(we used the Co-op, so that was posh for us),
no longer shin-kicked in the playground
nor standing up to street-wise evacuees
but, like frisky puppies calmed,
gazing up at His and His Dad's radiant features.

I think I'm more certain of *where* Paradise is.
When Farley and his wife went Antipodean
 and (compared to me) grew rich
from a motel and an avacado farm,
he begged me to follow where he said trees grew
twice as fast and twice as high,
'the moons of Jupiter are clear to the naked eye.'

Both of us were in search of the one thing
we had seemed to see clearly and then lose,
but that we still carried inside.
Our scraps of insight – trees against sun or rain –
that widened in the mind to greater miracles;
our deep Familiars.

2.

My Paradise was where my wife and I – suburban innocents
sniffing Sixties' liberties – fled

to Billy Ferret's (I'll call him) hillside farm
above the Pennine, cotton mills.
Water from a well. No electricity nor town-gas,
no rubbish-clearance, sewage, but a 'soil cart' coming round;
and (I think) our last lime-washed interior in England.
Two stone-floored rooms, two more above.
We'd little furniture.
A rocking chair, cost 3/6.
A bed from mother-in-law.
Outside our window, the majesty of cows
drifting home with swollen udders
and on the next morning seeking grass
grazed us with their wistful looks
that Hardy might have ascribed to Tesse.

But most important was our half-acre,
self-sufficient, organic garden.
Now that one can hardly find
a journalist who hasn't tried living off the land
or spent a gap-year in Provence
and only chavs don't buy 'organic',
it's difficult to recall that it was not in fashion;
an anomaly then to the nineteen-sixties,
called 'escapist' and backward-seeming.

*

Ours was a ground that needed to be *broken*.
'Oats in your first year, potatoes in your second
and in the third year thou mi't get a tilth,'
Ferret told me, 'But tha'll not grow nowt but grass up here.'
His three wild daughters agreed,
so did his bothered wife.

I went straight for the spuds and shall not forget,
when the tops were yellowing (I learned to wait for that)
my own crop rising out of the ground

like eggs so newly-laid
they've hardly formed a shell, are soft and white
and still internal as a mammal's foetus.
No need to peel them. No need even
to rub the skin off, as my father had
to show that they are fresh. You could smell them,
so lovely in their pale innocence
until shaken, when the nest of dry soil
cosseted in their fibres fell from them
and they dropped from their roots.

*

       At dawn I might be out
sifting compost through my hands:
the sweet product of earth-closet
(I ignored the 'night soil' cart)
and pig-shed and, (to give it heat),
layered with green nettles scythed from that bank
of rejoicing birds by the stream.
A four-week cycle.
I piled it up; I watched it sink
and steam within its wooden bins.

Or I drenched myself in the cream light
that came as suddenly as an attack
through flowering hawthorns.

Out in the first simmer
of bird-call that began each summer
day and that before many had passed
turned into a fever:
the perfect note blown time and again loud
from the deep breast of robin and thrush.
This world in its changes is Paradise enough,
its glide of seasons beauty enough,
I thought.   All youth's moments,
once reaped in fragmentary escapes,
had gathered here in a day by day,
rhythmic intensity.

I was drunk on the colours of flowers;
on the sweet deliciousness
of simply paying attention!
I seemed to draw birds out of the sky
down onto my sight, they were so vivid.
Observing it was Heaven to me.
The feather-flutter
of birds electric with apprehension;
or the weathering of a post
changed, as good things are, by time
to what is as differently fine
or maybe better.

Sometimes I felt all eye, all heart,
all love. Some trick of the light –
some *trickster* of the light –
among the hawthorns, say, would claim me.
Winged away
it seemed I'd always lived and would for ever
live in that stilled second.

Yet, under the hawthorns and around the sheds,
I'd brood on my fall into weak unhappiness
after friendship with Farley seemed passed.

II.

1.

Frustrated farmers lusted after her,
hung around smelling of cows and dogs
or came spruced for a dark evening,
stinking of after-shave, strangled in ties;
in wellington boots through mud and cow-slop,
with torch or hurricane-lamp, and an excuse,
as unguarded as children in their yearning

for my young wife's art-school patina.
Strolled out of their way down the path nearby
the pond and the wild hawthorn hedge.
Chatted as if casually with me at the gate.
Admired my garden patch on a bare hillside –
the beans' pendulous lamps of crimson flowers;
spinach, potatoes, tomatoes everywhere
grown wild from seeds in pig-manure;
or my canvas, though they'd one eye on the door
beyond which she too painted and dreamed.

Or I came from my garden (tasting the raw
delight of peas or radishes in the sun)
and against the scree of coals
piled in the shed that formed a porch to our door
I'd see his eyes, his teeth (if he had some)
and his generous-bodied lean:
a casual attitude of physical hope
I envied and admired.

I thought that I too would grow experienced and old
as some of these had; with a tough rural face
from endurance; cheerful lines, strong hands.
Not trained for it yet wanting their lore of hands.

2.

I crossed fields that were in a different mood each day,
their flowers upright or in decay,
and by dark sheds scary with sow or boar
that one always took a pitchfork to.
(Its motionless pause as if dead –
but keep eyes alert for that spidery lunge!)
Its stink of urinated straw.
The mare's upturned cart that she pulled the milk churns in
(and us sometimes on rainy nights to dances).
Instead of fields, I might follow her track

down to the hollow where a trout always sat
fanning its gills over pale stones
among rainbows in the water, that fanned it;
if not one trout then another, under wild thorns:
its station.   Next, up the slope
to a farm on the lane, from there to bring back
rejections of my poems, some acceptance.

And letters from Farley.
'A brake on an express train' was his view of women
who had persuaded me to 'a lesser course'
than our dreamed-of, organic colony
of artists in Borrowdale, Shropshire, or Wales; that plan
born of D.H. Lawrence and Ouspensky.
Should our friendship have been
lost – he asked – for a woman's dream?

I hurried back anxious about who sat at our fire.
Harry Crowe who lived with a dominant mother?
Another whose wife was as dull and old as he?
Billy Ferret himself? A scraggy mountain-dweller,
small, bright eyes of weasel or stoat,
never quite clean, living from thirty acres,
bothered by broken fences and three daughters,
daily carting to the end of the lane
his two full churns in a milk-float.

Though guarding my wife, I loved this man
who taught me to scythe (though never as good as he,
or if as good, without his endurance)
and to be midwife to his cattle;
sometimes calling me at night to a flickering lamp
in barn and cow-shed – where Rembrandt (partly)
had led me to observe among shadows
the metaphor of figures trapped in pools of light.

Or helping him squint into *The Farmer's Weekly*
at news of what was happening too distantly
to bother him much — but it scared me,
the galloping pace of intensive cruelty-farming;
all creatures from poultry to cattle crammed into cages
their short-lives long; asbestos sheds, demolished hedges —
the wreckage I already knew we'd not recover from
announced hardly-noticed in the farmers' paper

until it spread — it seemed to spread —
from there throughout our corrupted lives.
Bank loans and foreclosures
swallowed what simple farmers paid for.
The factory sheds and machinery ('plant!'),
groups of 'investors' for huge government grants took on;
England was wrecked (it happened too in France),
and most of wild creatures we depend on, died.

3.

One morning I invite him out to watch grass grow
and I tell him, my wife's pregnant.

You can spot the small finches in the grass;
then, not. But a month later still the crows
are seen to stalk on high-heels through the flowers.

'It'll not be a lad!' he laughs, shaking his head.
'Yon cart'll shake the tassles off a lad!'

I could tell when the grass was long enough for cutting,
for birds one only heard ran through it.
I think they were birds — you'd never know.
They only ran, calling, as if a gate swung on
stiff hinges, or thick oil was somewhere dripping.
'Ten shillings it's a boy,' I laughed. (As much as our rent.)
'It'll not be a boy,' he repeated. 'Yonder milk-float...'

For weeks he stared at grass. It must have been for hours
that he judged the field and that his eye
measured the overnight mist that stretches it;
as if he weighed grass palpably in his hands.
And weighed the weather.   Week by week, the gamble.
'I'll start tomorrow!' The neighbours laughed.
'Thou's wanting patience. Wait another week.'
'I'll get two crops if I cut it now.'
They laughed again – knowing that he never
made it before his grass grew rank with rain,
that 'second crop'. (Like his life, perhaps.)

Weeks of tension. Then at last
if there was a moon he'd be up at dawn
to scythe a wide, perimeter path
for his mowing machine around his first three acres,
waking us with the scent, and the satisfying rasp
when he paused to sharpen.
(Did that sound enter my wife's womb –
as they say that music listened to does?)
Next we oiled the mowing machine
that had rusted in a lean-to through the winter.
Sank hay-rakes in the cows' trough
for wooden joints to swell and tighten.

At the next dawn – dew still on the grass –
with an ecstatic glance at meadow and sky
he rushed through milking, tackled up his horse
and exhausted it: fanatical – and I'm not lying –
as Picasso, or as Montgomery in North Africa.
And when the grass is laid, his troops join the fray
to turn it in the sun (unless it rained) –
wife; his daughters, hopefully in bikinis;
and me. Not my wife, though.

He was the first I told: *I have a boy* –
and learned what kind of betting man he was.
So sullen – envious – I *never* dared ask for that ten bob.

4.

I can think of no metaphors for my love of my wife.
Maybe *love* is not what youth knows!
Love calls for experience, tested by trials.
What youth has is passion and promise
for that knife-edge of illusion which love must survive
by good luck, accident, or the timely kindness of friends
or even parents' good judgement (in the old days
when they were not mere 'wrinklies' but thought wise).

Wasn't I as much outside my own life with her
as the farmers, or as the passing cows!
I – though a father (shadowed by our child
that I looked at with a hypnotised stare,
time-stilled – is this the miracle I'm responsible for?) –
knew nothing of women,
had experienced little more than their power:
a chill with no more substance than a felt wind

and had drifted into a mad desire
for an amalgam of nature and woman.
(Anne Wylde, 'Hawthorn Goddess', I called her later,
maintaining her stubborness against the tides of men.)
An imagery that left a real woman stranded.
I saw the fire of her painting die and her heart go
as it can out of women misunderstood by men.
(Though I should have known this from my mother's
turning to drudgery, and forgotten piano).

*

It is hard to recall my love now that I feel cursed
for not being my wife's 'lineaments of desire' –
her inner man. Not sheathed as she thought in gold,
but the more sordid pig's-piss and manure,
cow shit, compost, grovelled earth;
clothed in the stink I love of barn and bog
that all who love the land must love;
that putties the curlew's feet when it springs,
as important for its wyrd call as the sky
when it cries *'Tell me! Tell me! What is lost?'*
(Listen when it planes up, planes down off the hills)
and holds it, when it comes back, fast.

I sometimes fancy that the darkness
that overwhelmed us was from those now built-over fields
where we, seductively though not fulfillingly,
arms round each other's waists, she in a batik dress
as enjoyed by art-students in those days,
and I rebelliously without tie, in 'sports jacket',
had often come to lie among wild flowers.

For what had those huge, ominous earth-shifters,
roaring and fuming, been turning over
as they bit into the fields and woods?
What dark gods – what augur for us
that the house of Brady and Hindley
(child-torturers and murderers, you will remember)
was built there?   Also, uncannily, Shipman
desecrated the ground of our tentative love?

5.

Even in earliest childhood, I'd found:
throw your thoughts out to nature, they'll come back gilded.
So today I leave my chair

for the autumn wood's stupendous gold and I think:
though we haven't exchanged a sentence in forty years
(a few clipped words but not a sentence)
yet such as this this we shared.
It could be this moment, this beauty
inspiring many an embrace against a world
that did not seem to understand.

We *could* have shared delight, you know.
My fault.
I still had to fight out of the dark –
as last night's dream of you does
with you more perfect in maidenhood than you were
and all was fresh about you,
eyes and hair warm brown as a native squirrel
or as the fields run to seed and sorrel.

I should have adored you as I did the fields
and their wave after wave of the
eternal ephemeral.

Instead I can only write of you in language that comes
as you do, from afar.

PART FOUR

I.

1.

My childhood had ended with burnt roses.
Youth finished with our first motor-car,
a vehicle we cyclists had abhorred
now bought to save, perhaps, a marriage.

And Ferret would no longer speak to us.
Travelling to escape him – and ourselves –
we became car junkies with lost bearings,
far from what is now termed 'holistic'
(and soon wasn't everyone
other than Innuits and Aboriginals?)
Our garden, sunk in weeds,
was abandoned (like my father's) in despair.
The ducks' throats cut. The poultry strangled.

Physicists tell us that some atoms' end
is to be burned down to lead and that was how
the molecules of our love burned down
to a dull weight in that decade
when shiftlessly we shifted with our child
through cottages on the Pennine hills.
(Gardenless stone-sheds mostly, furnished
shabbily by landlords). Both of us wondering
where our souls had vanished.
Had they lacked scaffolding? Or gone underground
on travels whose only point was to escape; or in arguments
dizzied by the cliffs and falls of love
at the desperate end of marriage?

Each marriage has different pains with which to end
and I'd known nothing like that one of her eyes
caressing another. She the first, lost garden of my soul.
I cannot blame her yet I seemed

suddenly to breathe a different air,
one dank and grey and stale.
Could love be anything but loss,
or be dreams felt more strongly than life
yet hardly spoken of? (My parents in my thoughts.)

Happiness now was when I posted my poems,
beers afterwards with a friend
or solitary rambles (that were conversations,
or rather piercing jealousies, in my mind.)
It was curlews arriving on the moor
announcing Spring with their high cries.
Pleasure in snow. Delight in a stranger's eyes
caught hopefully in street or pub.
(So many were clearly famished for love.)

*

But the most of what I seemed to have
was the grace of my telling. It settled on
the hills around us and their images –
those Pennine moors as restless as the sea,
a focus for winds and torches of shifting light;
the pearl sky mirrored in wet grass.
Their clattering steeps were a joy to climb
out of industrial clamour,
say to the top ridge of Hell Hole Rocks
(not to be wandered in a high wind).
See valleys like an emerald Psalter
opening their bright pages among the gloom.
Valleys worn by glaciers, then worn-out by weavers.

On rambles I followed the old causeways –
miles of paving two clogs wide.
Miles of stones on end, at one time flat,
now scooped to a long trough by the wear of clogs,
iron-tipped, trailing twice each day
between the farms and the weaving-sheds;

worn by children who travailed at mills and farms.
At one time there had been crowded lines of girls
on winter days through fields and woods with lamps.
Gathering at bridge or gate, they sang, they laughed.
Yards had been scrubbed, hens and beasts fed
before they descended to the mills
and I still hear them singing in the woods.

Now there's not much more than one lone hiker.
How many thousand miles have I walked
through a lifetime wondering who I am –
(what luxury) – to reach at last
four-fifths of an answer
on the verge of it being over.

2.

Grey light and bleak weather were my soul's
emblems in this second exile.
Lost friend, lost wife, lost vision and lost garden
helped me to understand the spirit's
historic starvation in these parts.
Loss seemed at that time the universal mind
begun at the First Garden, carried on
through the building of northern mills
and with those factories for souls called 'chapels'.

And the poor farmer among his sheds
going about his business without charm,
with his litter of wrecked machines, his mess:
sluttish remnants of the enclosures
that pleased the traveller Daniel Defoe
glad to see no spout no spit of water lost
out of the 'waste' by thrifty clothiers,
no blade of grass not turned to account.

I wrote much about him, his inner dark,
or light, whatever it was in which he lived,
that – like the homes they rarely let one into –
had to be imagined.
I faced the wet hills and the cold
with a stubborn bluntness
like his, I thought, my thoughts as his
who performs his immemorial acts,
digging, shovelling, calling of cattle,
that once were ritualised in fact
and blessed with higher, at least less squalid meanings:
the lit candle carried into church
as into a barn; wax the body of Christ,
wick the spirit, and the godhead, light.

*

Often I climbed the hills early, free
to see light break into a dove-soft morning,
the town below in strands of grey
and bird-flocks eager to feed
grateful it seemed for warmth –
such cackle or song, it was their world.

Often the electric, instantaneous
joy returned upon the sheep-cropped turf;
print of curlews' feet upon
warmly scented mud in the Spring sun.
Or when the sleek muscles of the hills
received their everyday miracles:
swathes and shards of light
skimmed off the Spring-touched fields,
as a conjurer's sleight of hand for secrets revealed.
And when the storm-filled rivulets
roared silver through canyons, joy flickered
on and off – a short-circuited switch.

Is beauty, the projected soul?
Or a veil of desire, that the soul throws?

3.

Yet in a perverse sacrifice of what I loved,
I fled – 'more liberated than my father' –
but came to disarray
and foolishness: one of that least wise types – young poets
with little conscience, few human skills, just verse,
plus sexual, alcoholic and other hubris.

*

A couple of bedazzled Northerners
were me and my mate Rogers on the Kings Road
where Northern lads were popular.
Were we Liverpool or Yorkshire? They could not tell
the difference, they – what was the phrase?
'Trendy'? No, 'with it', I recall –
mini-skirted barmaids who seemed to think
we must have been at school with Lennon.
I had an agent and a publisher then
and loved the busy way they shuffled scripts,
judging a writer's whole life dream
as they spun around London as fast as flies
giddying round a light bulb.
It also helped with sex
that I had published and 'gave readings'.
Yet my friend John was worse (or was it 'better')
at picking up, and getting us invited
with our carry-outs to parties
most often held in midget bed-sits
but sometimes with posh totty in big flats.

In my case looking not for a fuck but for love;
the love, or the several,
(the real and the imaginary) I had lost;
at once feckless and idealistic,
as Byron was. (Though not as handsome,
my gift of tongues made up for a lot.)
Sometimes I did fall in love,
while John went back to his regular bird
who photographed cancers at the Royal Marsden
and decorated their windowless, cellar-rooms
(let improperly by a janitor in Notting Hill)
with what looked like Beatrix Potter fungi:
crimson organs like lurid toadstools.
(And who took me into Biba for the fun
of showing me its loveliness and freedom.)

Then shoot up motorways in our mini-vans
for weekend 'access' to our kids.

II.

1.

My feelings when I had first climbed a hill
taken by Dad to Buxton on a bus,
aged ten, and when I first *owned* a home
aged thirty (the one that I am still in now)
were the same ones. Ecstasy pumped my breast;
enlargement bursting a cage
with an airiness not to do with cages
but with a trust in self
as I prised nails from the door and planks from window-panes
of a wrecked cottage, in a wrecked place,
bought for fifty pounds. (More than I could afford.
I borrowed his holiday money from a friend.)

It was not ruined farms and mills, nor stony roads,
nor Pennine grime that drew me.
It was at first my needing a cheap home.
Also, what I still adore:
that stream and then those woods beyond
that are now my daily altar
embroidered with their shifting threads, gold silk, or blue.

Instinct had assured me that I'd find my home
walking the hills in flight, if I trusted enough
under summer's curlew-cry, or in the snow.
Indeed I've lived here longer than anywhere else:
for more than half of my life.

2.

On my first night in Mill Bank, a starred night of frost,
I shivered in sleeping-bag on a dusty floor;
for company, my coal-and-wood fire's embers
that had dried the soaked chimney and had burned old nests.
Having fled with only what I could carry,
for months there was nothing there but what I needed,
could make, or could afford
by scavenging mill-sales or demolished houses.

My bare, new start.
            I was alone.
                        The moon sliding
westward dipped into the hills
beyond which my 'access' time was each week filled.
But that was a distant life now, and my dream is revealed.
Bare wood and a stone floor.
Wooden chairs that Van Gogh might have chosen.
A place in which to feel, not soft, but firm;
uncushioned, strong.
Here I was *at home* – at night to read
the Books of Martyrs – Shostakovich, Mandelstam;

the lives of the helpless, shuffled millions
of that and of all other centuries.
From them I learned in a bright epiphany
that it is enough to wander the lanes
and to live without suitcase packed for the knock at the door.

I began – I hoped – to be anchored at last. Have I come
to love this place as much as any woman –
or even more?   It has felt that way.
Though I kept on dancing with my frail friends
(or rather, it was I who was frail, more than they)
had the fox and the curlew become my kin?

3.

Here was not only a house to bring back to life
but a Pennine village, abandoned
in post-industrial hopelessness
to a few who clung to their past.
Then had come drifters;
outcasts and non-payers of rents
into the empty homes – though still
leaving many to silts of rubbish, and rats.
They were followed by us who were called 'hippies'
with our rough fondness for the stone cottages,
rented for a shilling, purchased for little more.
We'd tumble into them late at night
(into whose, no matter) from the public house
with our 'carry out' beers, and listen
to Blues and Beats; Billie Holiday and Dylan.
Then ten miles to Bradford where we'd go for curries
at dawn, or went poaching trout –
under the culvert, in the wood –
line wrapped around a finger, and a can of worms,
for small brook trout; not rainbows, tasty brownies;
five with bread would make a breakfast.

This got you called a 'hippy'.
Among grey, grey-coated ghosts of the past life
who saw no future in what they had given themselves to –
given lives, and their lungs also –
leaving empty homes as they sifted to the grave –
and 'a cold hearth'
with no children staying to warm the ashes –
we were incongruous, no mistake about that.
Newcomers who cheered the place up, nonetheless.

And in this place where gardens were not kept –
no point in fighting soot – now with the mills' filth ceased,
my other madness: in memoriam to my Dad,
against my wall I planted climber roses.

PART FIVE

I.

1.

We would rise and make love out of the sea;
my Greek, second wife, and I.
Imagine a heat where nothing moves
except the sea's blue and spray that fell from us.
Though day and light must have increased and declined
yet I did not perceive it nor
see change of life nor shadow on the herbage
nor clouds, nor colour beyond the blue,
much blue, and varied gold and white
nor sound beyond the even murmurs
that therefore was no sound,
of insects in far trees beyond the sand.
And out of this silence from time to time a lunge
of the sea lifting, weary, anyway gentle,
feminine I would say, strong, graceful
with a rhythmic mounting then a falling back
that Yeats might term 'a shudder in the loins'.

And we two making love. I'll not describe that.
Who can? Only before and after are we aware.
Metaphors will have to do. Those images I have described.
The sea still heard, from behind our rock,
in perfect rhythm for us, its sigh and fall,
but endless, heard after we had tired
no not tired but emptied – shared exhaustion's bliss –
and slept in one another's sandy arms.

Wake with eyes turned from the truth
of light. Kiss salt from off her hips.
Naked on this beach she's divested
of her bird-bright elegance from *Harrod* or *Biba*,
Paris or London, but not her beauty.
These images I retain today: Elleni's pearl skin

and long, Minoan waist
that I'd only seen in Cretan sculptures:
pale stone, like her flesh, unreddening, smooth,
delightful to trace one's fingers on –
and one's lips, if museums would let one do it.

After love she's detached. Yet not detached, really.
With an inner stillness.
Men are thought to be so too, but I never was
any less aware nor desiring of her.
Truthfully, she was more aware of me than before – just not looking.
I wanted it to last for ever
and little, if I'm honest, did I feel more than that,
not consciously.   Of course I did take in
her beauty (that again) carrying towels and her beach-bag
by the shore of that thrilling leap of the sea –
the pale foam sprinkled, then dying away –
strolling long-legged for a beer
(that is, an Amstell for me, for she drinks water)
for *psomi* and *octopothia*
under a cane-roofed, light-dappled taverna
where the northern tourists have arrived
(for this is early nineteen-seventy-four)
basted with sun oil for the roasting.

Though the quality of a moment at the time
has sometimes escaped me yet I knew
that this was happiness at aged thirty nine –
more than I'd dreamed of at twenty. (And fitter, too.)
Did I deserve such happiness
of being given to, like this, and loved like this?
At that time I assumed it. Now, I think I didn't.

II.

1.

When did love start?
Was it when hit by the glamour of her life:
an international shining, first in Hammersmith?
I appreciate more today how much she'd loved
the King's Road and the West End Theatre
when bursting from the narrowness of Greece.

Though it's the time of 'the three-day week'
yet power-cuts restored the world to our eyes,
for one could now see the stars!
Which is as far as we know the Universe.
As I was driving from Yorkshire to London:
maybe the Universe was advising clear-sight and caution,
with a petrol shortage? But love's not that way.
You find you're thinking only of what's in your –
what? Your head, soul, spirit, or your cock,
or fluttering in your stomach or weakened legs?

There seemed no place I'd stop in pursuit of feelings.
But what you know is, in love you're a different person,
one that you hadn't guessed you were,
one maybe better or maybe worse, but clearly
there are as many selves to be as there are loves.

2.

My first sight of her had been as a stoat's dance
(something I've witnessed); me the crouching rabbit,
victim of wandering into her gaze.
'Have you ever been to Yorkshire?' I kind-of idly asked
at our first, London meeting. 'I'd love to,' she said.

The stoat is dancing, in her Biba dress
like a spark, like a light bulb's filament
and I am crouching meat, already
thrilled by the first leak of my own blood,
ripped already by the stoat's teeth of unreason,
enslaved by the hope of affection – even of love –
and by the weekend's prospect, the food I'd buy in,
the flowers to arrange around my cottage,
the clean sheets and a fire in the bedroom grate.

Once more was it my task to make a life
out of found bits: the driftwood
warped by mistakes that one cannot explain?
Out of a past that she does not know
and out of the sea of two lives
wondering if one can – one possibly can –
build a hearth and shelter.

*

For her I think it had been my explosions of ecstasy.
It might be for bars of light between trees,
bright as medieval cloisonné. Or my staring
at each wave-advance of the Greek Spring,
orgasmos physos – 'nature's orgasm' –
when daily changes rose out of Africa
and drove northward over the Mediterranean;
cyclamen, anemone, flowering on sea-rocks.
Out of the soil-clutching cracks,
breeze-bent were their flowers
away from the *rack rack* of the sea.
The purple flowers of rosemary.

'What is he staring at?' her puzzled mother asked.

III.

1.

Stroll home through the hot streets.
Sometimes I felt there was little left of Greece –
as of many countries – but the ferocious sun,
sky-burn, and not even that as once: intensified,
raiding us from the skinned sky,
unabsorbed by miles of seaside concrete,
hot, windless, trapping petrol fume; the Parthenon
atop its hill, like a block of dried salt crumbling.
('A good place to view the Hilton,'
some Greeks say. They're proud of that!)

                    I thought:
there are beehives on that hillside,
not hidden, just tucked away
to catch the earliest sun and hold it
before it scorches; when the thyme is in flower
covered by trembling wings.
And many other 'English' blooms
in April, the month that finds it still too cool
to get quite out of bed, that goes half-dressed,
saying, 'Don't fuss, I'm getting there!'
out of every bird's throat – in Greece, the nightingales –
and out of magnolia flowers: such tarts in pink
spread-eagled against the wall.

To share it, I used to sit with those bees
(that should be proud because their honey
from Hymettos is the best in Europe)
when it was like my perfect English summer
and I would be flown home by that thought
to the deep moments of my boyhood.
(As Elleni too would conduct her ceremonies,
lighting up my northern village with
Sotiria Bellou and Theodorakis).

Yet Summer had to come. Blue day upon blue day
mounted on a bleached land rough with thorns.
Then memory of their calming hum
soothed me in the river of car-fume
that wavered in a simmering heat.

I was wearied by her desire for excess of light;
an erotic need of her pale skin
and fair hair (unusual in a Hellene) for sun.
She seemed not to want to know what shadows were
and showed an impatience for embracing them,
sensing they threatened her with northern dark.

She had to walk in the sun, I in the shade
and this was the source of one hot argument.
In Bouboulina, by the Junta's prison once
a nervous guard raised his machine-gun –
his cracked government being more frail
than our riotous yelling that we at last
resolved by walking on either side of the street.

*

We reach the flat where she changes after a shower.
Maybe a dress I'd bought for her. She's beautiful
(and I know how many times already I've said that)
and just as beautiful when she patiently bathes
her parents following their siesta.
(The time we had spent in the shade of the rock.)
Her passion for the passions of attachment,
family, love and loyalty was what she shared
with Antigone – her sister-darling. She like her
would be immured in Hell if love-faith called for it!

In this white room scattered with the sea-light's
silver leaf-dapple, little anchors me to myself
beyond clothes and books that are my own
and a desk before a window looking on

scented pines, the cones cracking
like gunshots under Mount Hymettos
(its marble pink at sunset and aloof);
papers, coffee cup, a glass of water;
the text of *Where I Used To Play On The Green* –
my first novel, trying to dramatise
spiritual maladjustment to the wealth of Nature;
and a typewriter retrieved from store
at the family's supermarket. (The typewriter
is a German Adler, grey,
and – shaped like a Second World War helmet –
it gave me eerie pangs of those old movies
we watched as kids in that war.)

Then there's her kitchen skills, her cooking.
Times when I valued our quiet bliss,
self-contained, say peeling an orange.
Sensuousness with food was almost strange to me:
bunches of grapes held over the mouth
or one another's mouths as in some pictured Bachanal.

*

Exquisitely even today lie tomatoes in my fridge;
exquisitely remembered. Washed fruit in a bowl.
What demon made me dissatisfied? I still do things …
her way of peeling oranges …

                      Thirty years later,
three marriages, and more loves gone by,
in Yorkshire I am cleaning radishes –
sun on the house front and a cd playing.
Leaving a curl of feathery leaf
and all of the rosy skin that is without blemish,
I recall the immaculate grace with which this was done
in Hammersmith and in those apartments near Athens.
The scent of basil, chamomile, rosemary,
and, seeping through an unglazed jar,

cool water with an earth smell fetched from Hymettos;
from the monastery among the irises
where Byron daily rode to write.
And her lithe father, eighty years old, dancing;
her mother of the same age wringing
her hands yet pleased by his laughing.
I made *her* laugh by mimicking Chaplin,
swinging my cane along a beach road,
and by imitating President Karamanlis.
'Greek men and women, I am the saviour of Greece.'
Conservative, genteel, yet she's primitive enough
to compliment me for making her daughter happy
with my soul, my spirit, and my penis.

What is poetry other than memory?
I lay the radishes – memory's scarlet eggs
hatching into their green, phoenix feathers
into the nest of a white dish –
in the same way she made beauty of each marital gesture
and of domestic living, a state of grace.

3.

It proved temporary as Harrod's Christmas lights.
When thwarted, vengeful as the Furies,
with the illogic of the Great Earth Mother.

I recall her manner, more than her words
in maddening arguments. (Her mindslip already beginning:
clutched knuckles tapping her brow,
tap tap, as if to wake some thoughts from there).

*

In an abandoned typescript I've not looked at for years
I find my account written with an autistic rage.
(This was after she changed the locks on my door.)
I scour the three hundred pages (before I burn them)
for insight, memory, or some clue
to what I felt then and this is what I found.

I knew that my marriage was finished
when what I loved had to be met in secret –
defended by my silence from her *caring*.
The Junta's and post-Junta's streets
were 'too dangerous' for me to walk
alone, not knowing the language,
and the countryside sizzled with vipers.
(Often one saw them smeared on roads.)
The roadside stalls were manned by cheats
selling poisonous snacks and Sounion's
cliffs were too dangerous for me, so I was told.
The sea beyond an invisible shelf
plunged into deep water where there roamed
sharks brought in by the American Fleet
that they'd followed from the Atlantic for the garbage.
(A metaphor in that, said left-wing Greeks:
'All that Americans brought us was sharks'.)
Her father (who from Peloponnisos
had braved Ellis Island, returning to Greece
to join an invading army, was captured by Turks,
enslaved to work in a pasha's garden,
presumed dead and, escaping to Athens,
founded a supermarket) thought I was mad
in my desire for the countryside.
'There's nothing but old people there!'
The old man laughed as few could laugh,
with his whole body, like a child.
What should I do? Stay in and watch tv.?

I stayed in with the tv though staring out
above the oven-hot pines
after doves in the early morning had coo-ed
the song of my longing in the bearable gold
of early sun over traffic's scream and whine
in the canyon where the earliest tanks
had ground up Messoyion Avenue to their barracks
and some walked to work in sandals.
Dappled by the unheated sun, they seemed free.

*

Often, to hear music, I walked the streets.
A piano that through an open window played.
I wondered – *is this fugitive me?* My appearance
was that of what she'd lied to her family I was
to show she'd made a good match – an 'English professor';
a northern Protestant who had discovered the South:
one of the bewitched northern artists in straw hats
(Lawrence, Delius, Hockney, Moore).
My shirts were washed and ironed by a maid
from Lebanon or Ethiopia. (Anyway, refugees,
always noisy and affectionate, it seemed).
I saw their aprons drying on balconies,
strings dangling, white starch glowing;
I saw their cheap and humble shoes
and thought of my mother.

Subtly I was changed, but they did not see it
or if they did, pretended not to and approved.
There's design in the kindness of the rich.
What is this comfort worth if I'm taken over?
Better by far to sleep under hedges.
My work was dying and a stubborn anger
replaced my generous thoughts.
I lapsed and then they noticed
my addiction to whisky, brandy, even Samos wine
(its sweetness Byron praised but I could not)

if there was nothing else as I worked through
bottles from 'our' supermarket arranged for show
in an Empire-style, veneer and glass cabinet –
since no-one but me was tempted by drink
and as this family was private, we'd no visitors.
(Though I preferred the despised retsina,
especially *apo barreli* – 'from the barrel' – with flies in it,
taken with chicken and chips in a basement caff.)
Immured in their business values – liberated, but not mine –
this new self, that I did not like,
was trapped on the edge of family observing
my wife's conflicts, serving and arguing
in a language I only slightly understood
(I hardly wanted to know what they were saying)
praising England (or, in England, Greece)
all to extremes; not getting what she wanted –
or rather what she is certain is right for all –
flying around (there and in my Yorkshire home)
like a parakeet with feathers on fire.

I'd sit with my whisky
on that penthouse balcony above the hot roar –
the dubbed tv in the corner, father-in-law
chuckling at comedies, brother-in-law
gloating at tv's Baywatch babes,
mother-in-law quaking at our threats to go out
(memories of the Gestapo in Athens and her son
picked up at random) and on balconies
at the far side of the street, the diners
almost close enough to touch, though not to hear
above the street noise; at the side,
canaries slung in cages – and I'd recall
shower-scented lanes in England long before,
the tree-overhung lanes muffled in wet,
while here they echoed in the heat
as if they were metal.

*

Sometimes I escaped to join the backpackers
who roasted, unwashed and salt-caked, on the beach.
Was tempted to vanish with these gypsies,
as were frustrated spouses in old tales.
I was envious of their casual island-hopping,
their sleeping on ferry decks and beaches.
Just to speak English, I'd buy them beers
or bring them home for a shower. I bridged two worlds.
Was shocked by their condescension
to the old lady; shocked with her
that they stretched their dirty sandals on our sheets.

I rambled the streets for days
through shaded canyons where the offices –
to stay cool, and private also perhaps –
closed their shutters and on balconies
the potted flowers were watered. No others idled like this
so I was thought to be searching for a whore
(brothels flourished for the siesta hours)
by sprightly pimps who called – when I shuddered off –
'I tell you Mister, you have complex!'
(Father-in-law laughed when I told him this.
'You should have said you want young girl, eh Glyn?')

Messages, money, even reels between cinemas
in those days were carried by men
with satchels – their dusty suits and their foot-weariness
recognised when they paused for coffee and water
mid-morning in cool yet sunny, ground-floor cafes,
in the clatter of backgammon boards
or the rustling of the pages of *Ta Vima*.
There I also stopped-by for my *apo barreli*
(for I was a messenger too, with poems though, not money;
nonetheless with something to bank).
I'd think of my family back in the flat,
the old ones watching tv from their beds
under their icons, the icon lamps glowing;

others arguing, and my wife
sooner or later holding her father's ankle
tenderly in the way that she did (ankle thick and strong,
arteries spreading their purple like a bruise);
laughing, easing their pains,
drawing them forth to give advice and be needed.
And I'd daydream again
of the green light under trees in England
or mantling them in a wet, English summer
with birds such as curlews, rooks or barn-owls –
you may hear them close and not see them –
skimming twilit mists.

The mind does this: condenses moments
for them to burn, it seems at random, later
without warning, through one's balance
that isn't balance at all, just temporary rest
in a chaotic flux.
                      My dear-achieved calm
settled in me: an anchor of iron or stone.

3.

By threat or blackmail, (*'I'm going home
to England – alone!'*) there did come escapes.
A boat through the Aegean!
Islands!

I was always taken by surprise
by the first buds of them on the horizon
breaking the calm pool of that blue,
floating on rainbows above a rim of surf
as if caught in the act of their descent,
not rocks from out of the sea.
They were so still beneath their perfume-clouds
of figs, oregano, and of thyme,
they seemed deserted. Then the cliffs

open and the noise of sailors
whose rhythms are the sea's, quick here, slow there,
waiting, rushing, tells us we approach a pier.
Nationalist music blares and there's the blue
phoenix and its soldier depicted in flowers.
(In years before the Junta fell, I mean.
Then they vanished and the police likewise –
or rather, they just swapped posts.)

The boat grinds its iron and we disembark
in the cacophony of those who importune
with that Hellenic gesture – from the breast
and open-palmed as if they held
their hearts, lightly though invisibly
about to cast them on the receiving air –
to let a room. My wife is good at this;
tireless, argumentative, persistent
and noisier than the 'peasants' as she calls them
who adore her certain air of money,
yet are, not just for her drachmas, welcoming.
Other travellers are confused. She, in her element,
flies up and down the lime-washed alleys
examining showers and rooms.
She's generous in her feelings, too.
She lectures them and they listen patiently:
on their history ... what to teach their children ...
how to clean showers ... and what to think.
How they loved to pour out their own stories too!
She, whose gift had been my first retsina;
the scent, the taste of origano;
earth scented with crushed figs;
gave also the delight (without being sanctimonious)
of consolation, holding the hands
of old people in their dusty beds.
She took in the appeal of their still eyes
in undergrowths of shrivelled lids and skin,
and answered with her joyousness.

(Once, following a mule track to the sea
through herbs and thistles and dry, wild wheat,
we came upon a house ... that man didn't even have shoes ...
and when I pulled off mine and gave them to him ...
though he protested ... he believed a saint
had been sent. But of course I didn't feel that.
I thought it would be nice to walk barefoot,
swim, buy more cheap shoes;
not envisaging the devastating sanctity
that truly came from her.)

*

When all is done, then on the sands
or walking to them through the olive groves,
through orange groves, by tomatoes and sweet corn,
through odours of oregano and of goat-crushed figs,
calm would settle, one in which one knows
time does not exist. We are in eternity
in the seconds of love, living fully.

Love is defined by this: *you are with someone.*
(Not waiting, or wanting to be.)
Physically, too. I tell you, I've never felt so lusty
before nor since.
And nature looks different to the healthy
who move with the taut rhythms of growth and flowering.
No sickly nostalgia setting one apart.

*

Yet I'd tire of playing the English 'milord'.
Enviously bumping once more into backpackers
(that made her lips curl with disdain
for their cheerful drunkenness and filth) –
as I'm a good walker (not a long stride
but good lungs, strong legs, and a light frame)
why did I not say: I'm going on foot

to cross the island, get drunk and sleep on beaches
with random company, walk back later,
or on the next day, probably?

Unkind to leave her, but if you'd been penned
as I had, you'd understand.
I could in the first place have come here alone.
Put my foot down, as you might say.
But at the time that had seemed not worth it
for there was such a price to pay –
though one that might have saved our marriage.

4.

That day I fled Greece they were arguing
about where to bake themselves on the hot concrete
by the sea during siesta hours. I refused to go.
(I'd heard too many family arguments.)
I lay cool and alone, the shutters closed.
Streamers of hushed-down sounds from far away –
or if not hushed, too sleepy, hot and tired
as goats and mules are in the afternoon –
reached me through the bleached stillness,
the rattle and the hum
of cicadas and other insects locked in pines
that nonetheless was the haunt of my English memories.
Why not go home? I thought.
Blind to all else then, I telephoned
the airport and there was a plane
refuelling on its flight from Kenya.
I packed my bag, I said goodbye to books –
my books falling apart in the dry heat –
and pulled the door locked shut,
quietly, for most were asleep.
Five hours later I called them from Heathrow.

For weeks I heard little but their tears
and, *'What have we done to you?'* I couldn't explain,
I couldn't (then) explain it to myself.
But I was back in Mill Bank. Home.

PART SIX
Hawthorn Goddess

I.

1.

On those days back home
coffee woke my morning, whisky completed night.
With friends, I felt the alcoholic's garrulous joy
until, when alone, it pitches into sadness
and the grip of every disparate spectre.
In the melancholia following drink
amnesia clouded, as in an animal's brain.

*

I imagined a feral spirit of this place.
She was of another time, the one of early mills,
yet of mine also. Abused and solitary,
draggle-skirted through her feasts of whinberries
that stain her lips, her shoes and dress,
their dye flows from her as she drinks the streams.

Or she lies safe where hares on ancient mounds
flee over wind-fiddled grass,
over wastes of cotton-grass and reeds;
she unseen beneath the tumulus rim. Or she is found
laughing on moorlands, or in a public house
lapping some brew in that harbour of stones;
gin, or 'black drop', or small-beer.
Or abandoned, in her wild foolishness,
to the dance, the clarinet and fiddle,
singing the song, the one I can't quite hear, of my home.

I write 'imagined', but she possessed a life
more real than what I thought of as my own
(but was not *her*s my own?)
One with me more than I was with myself.

She has kept me here since or has drawn me back;

the embodiment of those unconnected (were they unconnected?)
yearnings and desire for beauty distilled
out of trees, flowers, water, or the flux
of sky ... or from my inner self.
A pagan who lived as Christ said we should
on what was to hand; her pence from gathering berries
and roots for weavers' dyes perhaps.

I suppose that she herself could be composed of leaves;
her breath, the air and murmurs in a hedge,
her breasts those fruits and berries.
The wild flowers erupting from her flesh. Her song,
that crunched warble of the whitethroat
invisible in its loud fastness,
crushed, it seems, by the weight of green light
and not much more than an arm-stretch away
though its song bubbles out.
Yes, I could make her of this, that way...
sculpt, draw and write of her ...or she could be made
of nothing; made of light, yet made of everything
that matters.

Maid who had always been here, surviving.
The mills have poured their filth for a few centuries,
children malformed, the spirit deformed; no difference.
Telegrams poured home from the Front:
all of the manhood gone in one wave
from grieving streets.   No difference.

I saw her as most hunted when most needed.
I saw her embodied in an old, vague tale
which Imagination might fill ... a woman reviled
as a curse, though the curse was *they*
not able to accept this ghost of the past folk-ways
cast down to create her havoc
in mills and chapels of those days.
Preachers in their high-pulpit glamour

named her 'antinomian', 'of the Devil's tribe'
and even the 'true' tale from which I plucked her
aptly names her 'Anne *Wylde*'! The *Hawthorn Goddess*
of my novel of that name.
With her as companion I was not alone.

Memory of a Romany woman I had encountered
once out of the bogs:
a heretic – a cast-out – when I was a child?
So much she was me that I had become her lover,
more married to her than anyone 'real'.

2.

Something awoke me one moonless night...
the river's singing foam through my sleep,
or a river-dream wandering, perhaps. A voice;
and I was called to find her where she had been murdered.

Crashing through wood and stream –
the trees collapsing with elegance
in the slow dignity of autumn -
I was a solitary with one lit aim:
to go where legend says this had occurred.

I entered the unlit courtyard of The Dean.
Among tumbled stones and the deep holes
that had once been cellars – doors rotted on hinges;
old carts and stone troughs – an invisible hand
guided me with a bat's radar. Then, I was rooted.

Next was overcome by an invisible beauty
in the pitch-dark of a stage where the curtain has risen,
yet is empty for the tragic actress to appear.
Shaking, convulsed in waves, I was possessed
by ... not *my* cry ... for I was without control,
and it was not my voice but an inhuman call

torn out of an unsuspected well within,
quietly, then steadily louder.
At each attack I could bear no more.
Yet they came. Throat strained, I longed for quiet.
I did not know what frightened me the most:
the spasms, silence following, my violent shaking, or my feet
locked into the ground.

Then I moved. Regardless of my desires,
I dashed around the courtyard at great speed;
banged pitifully on abandoned doors
begging to be let in, to be freed
into what I had lost. What we have lost.

A moment's pause ... then off again,
shrieking, skewered on pain.
An ash tree confronted me in the wall –
I wrenched its branches off.
The first twigs did not satisfy
my occupying spirit so I tore at others.
Crushed branches on my head until I was soaked,
scented and cooled with moist leaves.
Now calm and happy, I laughed.
I roared that I was alive and had survived
and was certain of wonder! Paced up and down –
a wrecked, wet, but *unfrightened* being until I sank
exhausted on the cobbles.

Out of the dark there came a stone.
A smooth, oval egg, red in the rain light.
Not local stone, for they are grey. I clutched   ...
and suddenly all had gone. She was gone. The yard
was littered with torn branches of my madness;
worse, with dangerous spars and collapsed cellars
where I picked my way, again lost and afraid.

Someone, somewhere, had called the police:
I felt the moment. I clutched my stone
as headlights soon came to rest beneath the arch.
A policeman and woman on either side of the car.
'Put that down, sir!'   I calmly refused.
They saw I was harmless and they took me home.

Crazed with solitude, was I? Yes, of course.
Loneliness? Yes, that too.
Drinking too much? Yes, yes.
Crazed from dwelling on those gods of Greece? Yes.
Greeks saw us as shadows of the unseen gods –
which is to say, of our inner selves;
shadows thrown by the light of what we fear.

This too: my shrieks were ones that tore me from the past.
Its past. *My* past.
Its stone is laid on my windowsill today.

*

                      Another night ...
I cannot recall how much I drank
(and on the next day didn't count the bottles)
I went to my door and howled.
I wasn't blind-drunk for I could see, I think,
that I hadn't drawn forth the neighbours
(though probably they twitched their curtains).
I sank down steps into the street.
Midnight. Usually other crazed people about
crashing from the pub, or vans with thieves
(the coping stones of walls are often stolen,
so people write their names on them) – but none this night.
I shouted my progress while sinking down the hill,
throwing a challenge to an echo
not from houses but from hills and woods.

Again, I reached the stream.
What could be seen under trees was a washed green, steaming;
the dripping leaves weighed down;
and weeds in the choked dam that the stream fed
in wild joy before being harnessed.

I sat by the water and I cried at the dark
to call forth an oracle, spirit of here, 'Anne Wylde'.

II.

1.

I knew what had died. The place itself had died.
Not that I regret of course the cruel mills,
the blackened buildings and vile air;
harshness of materialism's single vision
and 'Newton's sleep' (I'm quoting William Blake);
Luddites hanged because they dreamed of bread
and equity; buried minds, buried 'hands' –
factory hands reaching out of the churchyards' mould –
or the wave after wave of bleak wrecks travelled through,
rising and falling before and behind the car
as one crests the troughs of Oldham or Burnley.
Nor even that they are no longer demolished
nor fired mysteriously in the night
for the insurance, or even out of instinctive hate
for being the cause of warped generations;
or in vengeance for poor Anne Wylde – to speak in myths.

But now that they have changed
into sleek apartments, does anyone hear
within them on a guilty, inner ear,
the cries of children maimed in machines
on those same floors (not oil-soaked anymore
but planed and varnished – skimmed of history's stains)?
Does anyone look in graveyards for their names?

(Those places of straw-dry grass, dogshit and JCBs.)
The brashness of a better life
had overcome my sanctuary and home.
The young executives and the first ranch-brains
had pulled down stone walls, put up wired
electric fences around bigger fields
for their trim horses. No sheep, cows, pigs, nor hay,
while farmers went off with their riches, happy
at what had evaporated – misery and grime.
But in the blather and speed of the changed valley
Mill Bank's womb of secretiveness had vanished.

Conquerors, who take not only the land
but erase graves and spirits
and even language wherein the spirit dwells,
change accent and dialect to another, mock as superstitions
the sustaining roots of belief,
had done better for themselves – but had done this.
I howled for what was lost;
for the voices of those within me that had died.
That book was over. That life, over.

And that inner woman who ravished my mind,
she whom I had not so much created as found
had vanished as in myth's prophecy I had described.

Aged, unrecognised by her own lover on the road,
back-bent, stooped out of her beauty, she had climbed
the horizon of history, to no grave. I described her thus,
(as one does without knowing when truly writing),
in *The Hawthorn Goddess*: not heard of again,
not even her bones found in a gulley after snows.
And I was primed for exile.

2.

Other ghosts trapped me in those days,
or nights. They were part dream, part vision.
Once I woke from a dream and out of shadows
through the starlight my mother dashed,
blade-like herself, and fast –
a bread-knife grasped in her left hand
in her second of hate that *I* could not grasp.
I recalled how she had done just this in the past.
Whether that was a dream-phallus in her hand,
or to castrate, I did not know.
I was not sure if I was awake, and she was real,
or had I dragged this image out of my sleeping?
Whether she had come out of my mind
or from some *mysterium magnum,* I could not say.

*

Or perhaps it was her projected jealousy.
For neither did I think of *this* at the time:
but after forty years I'd tracked Gertrude down
to an old people's refuge, and her flat
not one mile from the bus-depot and The Moss.

Black, her hair still – dyed of course;
a trimmed, old 'working class' lady.
This spirit of wild wet places was now part-civilised,
but no mistaking her surviving gleam
gay as a girl, eyes startled with hope
on behalf of the love-faith that was still there
and that made my stiff politeness not needed.

*'He promised that when you were twenty one,
he'd join me.'* (She did not add: *he lied.*)
*'Forty years passed and I neither heard nor saw
of him but for my photos,
except once ... there'd been some quarrel with you.*

He came round drunk and crying.
I did not even know that he had died
until told by Taffy Jones in the street.
'Did you know Inspector Ewes has died?' Taff said,
half way up Groby Road. 'A month ago.'
I didn't even get to his funeral.'

I thought of his fall against the bathroom door.
Did he think of *her* at that moment,
her image in his mind – did she wonder that?

I thought of those attendant bus crews
and she, his love, not there.
She'd have thought, and thought again, about that.

'I went home and cut up, then I burned his pictures…
Do you have any photos of him?'

'I have, I have.
May I ask….' I added ….
'Of course I won't press you, but I'd love to know…
Was the sex good?' I asked. *'Oh, it was, it was.'*
The gleam returned. *'So glad,'* I said, *'So glad.'*

PART SEVEN

I.

1.

Our offshore island was soaked in cold,
rain or ice and darkness curled like a black dog
on a black rug between horizons of light
as if it poured through gaps around a door.
All Europe was the same, I suppose,
its North anyway, its East maybe worse
with a bleaker vastness
this time of year; its pines, its museums and traces
of horrible camps that I've not visited.

I had such images as these
to match my state of mind in Eastwood, Nottingham;
cradle of D.H. Lawrence, if you've not thought of that.
For his Centenary I am 'Writer-in-Residence'.
Also, it's the year of *The Miners' Strike*.
Visitors were dismayed by this decrepit place,
its starved-out shops and housing barracks,
its vandalised graveyard with names found in Lawrence;
its worship of coal and of coal's murderousness –
worshipped even as the last pit closed that year.

Anger and chaos marched the shut-down town.
I stood near Arthur Scargill who was perched on a wall,
locked out of the 'Miners' Welfare' in the rain.
Unconfident yet bold, bit of a strut like my Dad,
and perhaps with a disguised sense of failure like my Dad's,
is that Union leader answering jeering hacks
but lacking the guile not to insult, not to be drawn.
Offering no more than not wanting the pits closed.

Offering no *inner life*, as he might have done;
nothing of that which Socialism lacks.
(Circumstance, I suppose, was not for that.)

Miners jeered from the 'Welfare's' windows and out of cars.
Some wanted the pits to stay ... also the deal
for closing them: those pay-offs spent on dreams
that were ruthlessly peddled from door to door
- house extensions, new cars, caravans, drives.
Then, nothing. State welfare.
What a defeat for my *father's* dream!

I wanted to take Arthur Scargill by the arm,
say, 'Come with me to another miner's home,
the Lawrence family's, where I happen to live.
Come – I'll light a big, coal fire – the Pit
heaps it free at the gate, as you'll know – and we'll talk.'
(The old miner next door who sleeps upright in his chair
or he'll drown in phlegm, spits, coughs beyond the wall,
yet wants the Eastwood of coal to last for ever.
Sometimes his family swamps his coughing with music,
marital rows and dog-bark.)
'I'll tell you, Arthur, how I learned what it is to be black
when – my accent overheard in a southern town –
insults were cast about you and the miners.'

This did not happen, alas.   A car took him away.
I returned alone, the Arts Council's solitary 'Fellow'
in that bleak, end-of-terrace house
(the staircase narrow as a pit):
twenty-eight Garden Road, a.k.a. 'The Breach',
furnished with Eastwood's cast-offs to make a museum.
In there was my functional, two-room flat
where Lawrence had lived-out 'Sons And Lovers',
and I could hardly compose a line for the ghosts
so like my own – possessed by a cold mother's
quarrel with a father of spurned strengths.

No words of mine from a desk in their bedroom.
Just my dreams, not quite recalled, of battles, of birds;
of alien countries, and lost keys.
Winter days grew dark again before they had grown light.

Most evenings I walked to the telephone box
(it's by the old Manor where the humiliated young Lawrence
was sent to collect his father's pay)
to call my home where my wife, returned from Greece
while I was away, had changed the locks.
Yet Elleni would sing as naively as a bird
of family …. of the Greek food waiting for me …
of archaic ideals that had thrust her back:
'You must follow your husband wherever he goes ….'

What's wrong with me? I wondered.   *Why must this happen?*
My mind was focussed on 'ifs'.
My life will change if that sky-scape does,
that cast of stars, that planet over the street
with its uncompromising shine like the gleam of a gun.
How mad was that?
And yet, with the planets, it did.

2.

Off Nottingham Road, top of Victoria Street,
(brick terraces line a tempting slope
down to a swathe of grey countryside,
its shine like gunmetal on this wet day)
there once was a shop where Mrs Lawrence sold lace.
I stepped inside and stood before the fire
lit in its black-leaded, brass-polished, shrine.
Only two of us were there.
(Though there was a third who toasted pikelets –
the museum keeper – only we two were there.)
Strangers but not strangers. You know what I mean:
how one registers mutual need
and later learns what that need is.

We did not sense … I do not think we did … the seed
of our coming frisson of loss and pain,

fertilised in the egg of love by that
consummation of our eyebeams meeting.
Nor did we see the start
of our Wagnerian ride upon the powers
of *eros kai thanatos* – love and death:
a self-consuming rage that destroys, and when it dies
is as cold and dull as it had been hot and bright;
the phoenix screaming on its ashes.

How apt for this was the place where we met,
or rather collided, in Lawrence's birthplace!
We were two arrows, she stopped in her flight
southward from the Calvinist North to Italy
and I blocked northward home to Mill Bank.

3.

Frolicking through our lazy afternoons,
love was cruelly more for that ring of pain
– her husband and children; mine, and my wife –
safe for us beyond our gambolling field;
no telephone troubling the bedroom there.
What were we thinking of, being so dazzled?
Nature and sex – what else?
But sometimes from so strong a desire
that it seems a need, part of one dies.
We should have been learning from Faust, not Lawrence –
as our dangerous hunger was not for knowledge, like Faust,
but for that terrible, lovely thing: feeling
(defying goodness and truth). Then paying.
I should have been warned by our first,
                                  Whiskey binge …

Hooked on mutual torment also, but we failed to see it:
so perversely blind in this delight;
caught in the web of a sensibility
without conscience, only frisson.
We should have remembered Faust

in our conspiracy, but our generation
thought it knew better than not to despise
the wisdom that 'duped' past ages.

The happiness we thought was real, was fantasy.
The darkness we thought of as fantasy, was real,
shaping our destruction, although it felt like joy
as never before – so highly pitched
and *seeming* all brilliance and all light
in those spiritually darkest of days.

4.

                and yet again to dream the journey
of love the way we made it.   Ways of love not felt before.
Fierce bites as if a swarm of wasps bit ravenously,
electric from head to toe, and kisses exploring.
Entrance that began for me with my howl
coming always into a well of air.
Why should a shout so unlike my own,
stronger than any normally – deeper –
as if another's – come forth at that moment?
if I did not howl she accused me of not loving her.

Sleep. Then wake to light of amazement
holding one another in the dark,
finding we'd dreamed the same dream often
or our matching parts of it. Then entwine
ourselves day after day into the same thoughts
so that we were happy only in the same thought;
soul-twins wrecking the bed in turmoil.

She asked me what I thought love was? I replied:
once, camping on southern Downs, I came across
two adders caressing. Heads to tails locked,
hardly moving yet at every point moving,
back and forth, head to tail and tail to head,
I stood three feet away with nothing to fear

for they were so absorbed; only envying
the sun-trap of sand that they had found.

Love is wholeness like that, I said,
whether we are together or apart.

5.

In two years when shut out of Mill Bank
began flights so suited to our genius.
Wearisome searching and not finding.
Yet it now seems our greatest happiness
(happiness though not peace, never peace)
was our exile in cottages, gathering sticks
for firewood from hedgerows in the snow
or measuring the acres of wild flowers
in Rutland and in Wales.
The apple and pear-tree planted, garden constructed
above the River Aeron
where sea-trout stirred in their lusty glide
- so certain – up, then downstream to the sea.
The lean-to where I wrote.
It seemed that all I'd ever wanted was that desk
(its calm so different to the confused book
I was writing about my experience with 'Elleni').
And *the* loved one. Muse three. Despite our quarrels,
'I admire it that you are always able to write,' she said.

Then swift darts on fast roads, lingering on others
to enter the oven of her beloved South;
short pauses, long ones, however it fell.
Green flames of apricot trees against the snow
of Pyrenees. Vineyards dressed in flowers;
olive trees and river banks with nightingales.

Flights marked by laughter or by brilliance
and by our Devil-may-care seeming bravery.
France Italy Austria Greece The Mani –
how briefly the names are spelled! Each day a lyric
to new life, or hope of life – not mere adventure –
as I felt our bodies ease into love
gently as a ripe grape melts in the mouth.

6.

By the time that my home was retrieved
my love had become an alcoholic
sometimes with gin bought at the post office
on helpless dashes that she could not resist,
swigged quickly then hidden in the airing cupboard
or elsewhere when she learned it was discovered.
As a bird that senses strange hands on its nest
or as a hare does, she hid what was most precious
and slipped the next bottle, say under the sink.

I would come downstairs to find her shaking and weeping
or staring out from the open door.
Once many emotions had ranged upon her face.
Now there was only that transfixing stare,
as if she could see Italy or France beyond the trees,
beyond my streams and hills, or almost,
or was deluded that, in trance, she did.
Poor shaking hands, poor shaking thing.
I'd kiss her – but to test if on her breath
was what I grew to hate: that sweetness
as of something rotting inside.

*

Separations next. Her blank postcards
were articulate silences from 'our places';
wherever there was that still trapped
in memory our frail, but there existing, happiness.
And many times to dream
that the lost one will appear at the lonely door.
I'd go in the street and expect to see her coming.
(And once she did indeed appear
for the meal I'd laid for two, not one.)
It was as if we were – well, no '*as if*' – we *were*
in a harmony that brought us symbols
and archetypes of our love and grief.

We met again and in a hotel lounge
fell in a storm of tears and joy. (A brief reprieve.)
'The eternal lost one,' I could say –
the one that in truth was many,
as my late mind sees.
One stuffed with moments, gestures;
hair of women, woodlands' scented sides,
and the sea stirring in some Greek bay.

II.

1.

Meanwhile, Elleni was stepping out of her mind
although I did not know it then;
I had forsaken the privilege of knowing her mind,
her maddening inconsequence, its beauty.
What, hidden, uncoded, was imprisoned there –
though outwardly showing forgettings, foolishness,
and confused opinions that confused our friends;
also market-traders shopkeepers builders tradesman;

later amusing care-staff in Athens, while her grasp
of daily needs slipped into the oubliette of her mind
there shape-shifting among characters, as they had
in her play that became a novel then a play
and then a novel again (I did lose track)?
Also, what thoughts were *sharpened* in its recesses?
I wondered years later when I heard she had died.

Among mutterings, or was it rages, or just silences,
I imagine her sifting the parts she might have played
among what memories she was still able to hold.
Soft rain of England that she had loved.
Or the glassy brittleness of sea
reflected in splinters, on white rocks,
when she bathed or writhed in her beautiful lust.

Until she vanished among nurses and perplexed visitors,
as Anne Wylde had vanished, as I had prophesied.
Or perhaps it was that she fell *into* her mind
with Alzheimer's? Into that storm
whose rage was cracking her beauty.
She might have felt it, but did not understand?

It is *my* ignorance that seems terrible now!
How I had betrayed her and deserved
                                        my nemesis;
also the ashes on which I left her,
so as to save myself and my *work*,
                                        haunt me now.
Oh why does not God let *us* be God sometimes!
Surely a moment of omniscience,
permitting us to love at a *useful,* not *regretful* time,
would not harm Him?   Surely
He's not cruel merely
to teach us the virtue of *regret?*

PART EIGHT

I.

1.

To show they endure, old men continue habits
exaggerating echoes of what they once were.
As during a power-cut one still presses switches,
or as one long captive loves his captors,
they persist in seeing what they thought they saw
long ago, say in the lilac flower
flourishing high above the gate;
captive still to an old beauty.

Often my mind returns
to where I have left some parts of myself.
Hayfields of boyhood, sun reflected in scents.
Air-glazed shadows of the woods
where I would allow my ecstasy to take over.
Winter anemones at Sounion
where the breezed wildflowers will dance for ever
on a cliff-top above the setting sun.
Summer on island beaches
and that wife's body rocking with desire
gold in the sun of a moment that was gold.

2.

We had believed – my friend, Farley and I –
that over the hill there was a Paradise;
beyond the horizon was a sensuous
Tahiti dreamed up by Gauguin.

Though Gauguin died too young of syphilis
(young compared to us, that is)
it still seemed heroic, a hope of faraway
that took Farley to New Zealand,

and me after forty years to see him –
as we had promised to meet at the end.

For me, a flight towards the rising sun
through almost-seamless dark
broken when dawns gleam and are gone,
blinds down anyway for another cretinous film.
Europe clinging to the fringe of Asia
skipped almost in an hour. A short day and a long night
of empty valleys and peaks. Dawn upon a frozen sea
but, when southward travelling, fishing boats.
Brushing my teeth in Tokyo.
The Pacific. Tahiti set among those
jade earrings circled with their foam;
perfect atolls uninhabited
except for USAF bombers perched
threateningly light, as huge flies on a stone.

I knew by then that there is no flight but theirs.
No escape but into the mind –
the hermitage of self, wherever one is.

3.

Now I find that the Paradise 'over the hill'
is the flower at my door
that makes one want to live after all.
Is the look I bring to bear on the fields
or the warmed scent that is Spring
and that since boyhood inspired my truancy.
Is that light in the trees
after weeks of rain, rain on the leaves
that sometimes shines like silver flowers.

II.

1.

Once from a flat roof in Greece
in something milder than a night-breeze,
more like the breath of goats settling to sleep
where they knew it would stay cool under trees
in summer-dry grass where the fireflies were,
I recall a universe crackling with stars;
some in streaming flocks
that burned out suddenly.

There I lay side by side with a friend
and as we talked, with not much to say,
just friendship that didn't require words
(at the time I was beginning to see, I think,
that good friendship is better than bad passion) we stared
upwards and both felt the vertigo
of tumbling through the Universe:
particles with no sense of ending, which we are.

Also one day by the Hodder, in its alders
I recall the gatherings of warblers
that broke off their song to moisten their beaks in the stream
dimpled by rising trout and grayling
while a summer's day
stirred once more its nuclear impetus
and a gold sheen of still-unopened buttercups
gilded the slants of morning sun
where a favourite meadow was awakening
again into sorrel and mayflowers.

Single days or evenings among thousands.
Why do I not recall all, in this vivid way?

*

Though I'm frailer now, will some person catch the gleam,
on some days hence, of one starting again
with a happier breathlessness than the one it seems:
not sickness, but the panting of a boy
once again waiting for beauty to alight at a station?

LIST OF SUBSCRIBERS

Anna Adams
David Annwn
Jenny Aveyard
Juliet Barker
Paddy Bushe
Sam Clare
Kevin Crossley-Holland
John Davies
Ronnie Duncan
Kenneth Eatch
Tony Elwell
Rev. Kevin Firth
Ian & Barbara Fraser
Justine Gaunt
Goldmark Gallery
Catherine Galvin
Rigby Graham
George Guest
David Hallgarth
David Hargreaves
John & Katherine Hart
Trevor Hoyle
Trevor Hyett
Albert Irvin
George Kelsall
Tony Knipe
Beate Kubitz
Andrew Lambirth
Colin & Anita Lounsbach
David Lascelles
Olivia Lousada

Celia Lyttleton
Andree Molyneux
Mac & Maureen Moore
Serena Nuttall
Eileen O'Brien
John Parr
David & Tina Pease
David Pownall
Jacki Proctor
Colin Raw
Sara M Rayment
Shirley Rayment
Tim Rayment
David Rees
Judy Rodrigues
Jane Rowlands
Laurence Ryan
Keith Sagar
Anna Scrine
James & Jocelyne Scrine
David Seymour
Mrs H Shaw
David Sim
Susan M Stephenson
Chris Sterry
Gilbert Ward
Rodney Watson
Gerry Wells
Ian Wheatley
Rodney Wood